MW01205924

GEMINI
2024

Zodiac world, Volume 8 Published

By Daniel Sanjurjo, 2023.
While every precaution has been taken in the preparation of this book, the publisher assumes no responsibility for errors or omissions, or for damages resulting from the use of the information contained herein.
Gemini Horoscope for 2024

First edition. November 22, 2023.

Written by Daniel Sanjurjo.

Introduction	6
Gemini Zodiac Sign	10
Gemini Personality Traits	11
Gemini Horoscope 2024	20
Gemini Love Horoscope 2024	24
Gemini Career	26
Gemini Education 2024	28
Gemini Career 2024	30
Gemini Education 2024	32
Gemini Finance 2024	34
Gemini Family 2024	36
Gemini Health 2024	38
Gemini Love 2024	40
Gemini Summary	42
Gemini Child 2024	43
Gemini Marriage 2024	45
Gemini Sibling 2024	47
Gemini Travel 2024	49
Gemini Gifting 2024	50
Gemini Business 2024	51
Gemini Property and Vehicle 2024	54
Gemini Legal Matters 2024	56
Gemini Wealth and Profit	57
Lucky Number for Gemini Zodiac Sign in 2024	60
Frequently Asked Questions about Gemini	61

Summary for Gemini - January 2024:   63

February 2024 Horoscope: Gemini Energies   68

March 2024 Horoscope: Gemini Energies   72

April 2024 Horoscope: Gemini Energies   77

May 2024 Horoscope: Gemini Energies   82

June 2024 Horoscope: Gemini Energies   87

July 2024 Horoscope: Gemini Energies   92

August 2024 Horoscope: Gemini Energies   97

September 2024 Horoscope: Gemini Energies   102

October 2024 Horoscope: Gemini Energies   107

November 2024 Horoscope: Setting Goals and
Facing Challenges   112

December 2024 Horoscope Summary for Geminis:120

What Are Geminis Into?   123

Geminis Attractive Traits   129

Who Gets on Best with of Geminis   134

Turn-Ons   140

Turn-Offs   145

Astrological Remedies   150

Preferred Gifts: 155

Adversaries to Gemini natives?   164

Gemini and Aries Overall Compatibility: 168

Gemini and Taurus Relationship Analysis   170

Gemini & Gemini: A Mirror of Twins   173

Gemini & Cancer: Balancing Differences   175

Gemini & Leo: A Playful Connection   178

Gemini & Virgo: Intellectual Connection with

Challenges 180

Gemini & Libra: A Meeting of Air Signs 183

Gemini & Scorpio: A Complex and Challenging
Connection 188

Gemini & Sagittarius: An Adventurous and Playful
Duo 192

Gemini & Capricorn Compatibility 196

Gemini & Aquarius Compatibility 200

Gemini & Pisces Compatibility 204

Gemini Man: A Lover's Guide 208

Gemini Woman: A Lover's Guide 210

Conclusion: 266

Contact Us 271

Thank You, 271

Dear Reader 271

About the Author 278

♊ GEMINI™

Introduction

Dear Reader,

Welcome to a fascinating journey through the world of astrology, a journey that promises to unveil the secrets, characteristics, and unique qualities of the Gemini zodiac sign. In this book, we invite you to embark on a captivating exploration of Geminis, their personalities, and their destinies.

The Gemini Horoscope for 2024:

At the heart of this book lies the Gemini Horoscope for the year 2024. You'll find detailed insights into what the cosmos has in store for Geminis in the coming year. Whether you're a Gemini or have a loved one born under this sign, this horoscope offers guidance, predictions, and a glimpse into the cosmic forces that will shape your life in 2024.

A Deeper Understanding of Geminis:

But this book is not just about predictions; it's about understanding the core essence of Geminis. Geminis are known for their dual nature, and we'll delve deep into what makes them tick. From their strengths and weaknesses to their likes and dislikes, you'll gain a comprehensive understanding of the multifaceted Gemini personality.

Exploring All Facets of Gemini:

In addition to the horoscope and personality insights, we'll also explore various aspects of Geminis' lives. From their compatibility with other zodiac signs to their romantic and professional lives, you'll uncover the full spectrum of what it means to be a Gemini.

Beyond the Stars:

While astrology gives us valuable insights into our lives, it's also a source of endless fascination and self-discovery. Whether you're a devoted astrology enthusiast or simply curious about the world of zodiac signs, this book offers a gateway to exploring the cosmos and its influence on our daily lives.

Other Zodiac Signs:

We invite you to explore the other zodiac signs as well. You can find dedicated books for each sign, all created with the same passion and dedication that you'll find in this volume. Each sign has its unique characteristics and stories waiting to be uncovered.

A Personal Astrological Journey:

Lastly, remember that astrology is a personal journey. As you read through these pages, consider how the insights apply to your life and your unique experiences. The stars may guide us, but our choices and actions shape our destinies.

Thank you for embarking on this astrological adventure with us. We hope you find inspiration, clarity, and a deeper connection to the cosmos as you read through these pages.

Warm regards,

Gemini Zodiac Sign

- **Element**: Air

- **Color**: Light-Green, Yellow

- **Quality**: Mutable

- **Day**: Wednesday

- **Ruler**: Mercury

- **Greatest Compatibility**: Sagittarius, Aquarius

- **Lucky Numbers**: 5, 7, 14, 23

- **Dates**: May 21 - June 20

Gemini Personality Traits

Gemini Profile: The Curious Communicators

Introduction: Gemini, the third sign of the zodiac, is celebrated for its lively and adaptable personalities. Those born under this sign, which includes individuals with birthdates ranging from May 21 to June 20, are natural communicators who thrive on intellectual stimulation.

Colors: The Vibrant Hues of Dual Nature Gemini individuals are drawn to colors that reflect their dual nature. Light-green and yellow stand out as the shades that resonate most with them. These colors symbolize their versatility, curiosity, and youthful energy. Light-green represents their ever-active minds, while yellow embodies their cheerful and optimistic outlook on life.

Gemstones: Agate – A Mirror of Mental Agility The gemstone that aligns with Gemini is the mesmerizing agate. Agate is known to represent mental agility and balance, making it a perfect match for Gemini's inquisitive and adaptable traits. Just as the agate encourages harmony within its various layers, Geminis maintain an inner balance that helps them navigate the complexities of their ever-curious minds.

Qualities: Unveiling the Essence of Gemini Gemini individuals are known for a range of distinctive qualities, each contributing to their unique personality:

1. Curiosity: Their inquisitive minds are always seeking new information and experiences. They are the perpetual learners of the zodiac, driven by an insatiable thirst for knowledge.

2. Adaptability: Geminis effortlessly adapt to changing situations and can connect with people from all walks of life. They are like chameleons, blending seamlessly into diverse environments.

3. Versatility: They excel in a variety of areas and have a wide range of interests. Whether it's writing and public speaking or art and technology, Geminis are often multi-talented individuals.

4. Communication: Communication is their forte. Geminis have an innate ability to convey their thoughts effectively and engage in lively conversations. They are natural wordsmiths, skilled in the art of language.

5. Youthful: Gemini individuals often maintain a youthful and exuberant spirit throughout their lives. Their curiosity and playfulness keep them feeling young at heart, no matter their age.

6. Social: They enjoy socializing and have a vast network of friends and acquaintances. Their charm and wit make them magnetic in social settings, and they are often the life of the party.

Weaknesses: The Flip Side of Gemini Alongside their strengths,

Geminis have certain weaknesses that are important to recognize:

1. Restlessness: Their constant need for stimulation can lead to restlessness, making it challenging to focus on a single task for extended periods. They're always seeking the next exciting thing.

2. Superficiality: Geminis' versatility can sometimes manifest as superficiality. They may skim the surface of various topics without delving deeply, as their curiosity leads them to explore a wide range of interests.

3. Indecisiveness: Their curious nature means they want to explore all possibilities, which can lead to indecisiveness when making choices. They can be caught in a perpetual cycle of weighing options.

4. Impulsivity: Geminis may act impulsively, making quick decisions that can sometimes result in unforeseen consequences. Their impulsive nature can be both a strength and a weakness, depending on the situation.

Interests: The Varied Passions of Gemini

Gemini individuals have diverse interests that cater to their intellectual and communicative nature:

1. Books: They have a penchant for reading and may often be found immersed in books or e-readers. Their voracious reading habits satisfy their never-ending quest for knowledge.

2. Music: Geminis appreciate various musical genres and may enjoy attending concerts or playing musical instruments. Music serves as a form of emotional expression for them.

3. Writing: Many Geminis are drawn to writing, whether it's blogging, journalism, or creative storytelling. Their natural communication skills find an outlet in the written word.

4. Travel: Their curiosity extends to exploring new places, and they relish short trips to satisfy their wanderlust. Traveling allows them to experience the world and gather new stories to share.

Dislikes: The Aspects of Life That Challenge Geminis There are certain things that Geminis are not particularly fond of:

1. Solitude: They thrive on social interaction and dislike extended periods of solitude. Geminis draw energy from being around others and engaging in lively conversations.

2. Repetition: Routine and monotony are their nemeses. Geminis prefer constant change and excitement, making them easily bored by repetitive tasks.

3. Being Confined: They feel stifled when their freedom is limited, whether it's in relationships or their daily lives. Geminis cherish their autonomy and value the ability to explore diverse experiences.

This comprehensive profile offers insights into the multifaceted world of Gemini, with a focus on their qualities, preferences, and aspects to be mindful of. Understanding the intricacies of this zodiac sign allows for more profound connections and interactions with the Gemini individuals in your life.

Gemini Horoscope 2024

A Glimpse into the Year Ahead

Unlocking the Mysteries of Gemini's 2024 Horoscope

The Gemini Horoscope 2024, as crafted by AstroSage, promises to be your guiding light, offering profound insights into the transformative changes awaiting the Gemini ascendants in the upcoming year. It delves into various facets of your life, from career and finances to matters of the heart, personal life, health, and marriage. This exclusive horoscope is rooted in Vedic Astrology, meticulously considering the planetary movements and constellations up to the year 2024.

If you find yourself pondering questions about the coming year, such as the direction your career is headed, financial prospects, the ebb and flow of your economic situation, or your educational pursuits, this special Gemini Horoscope 2024 holds the answers you seek. Dive in from beginning to end to unearth the wisdom it offers.

Your Unique Journey Awaits - Gemini Horoscope 2024

Charting the Path for Your Success in 2024

What sets this Gemini Horoscope 2024 apart is its tailor-made insights designed exclusively for you. Within its pages, you will discover a roadmap for the year 2024, offering accurate predictions and practical remedies to ensure a successful and prosperous year ahead. By understanding the influence of planetary positions and stars on various aspects of your life, you gain the power to plan your year with precision.

AstroSage's esteemed astrologer, Acharya Dr. Mragaank, has meticulously crafted this horoscope, taking into account the intricate dance of celestial bodies and their effects on your life. It's worth noting that this Gemini Horoscope 2024 is grounded in your moon sign, making it particularly beneficial for those born under the Gemini Moon sign or birth sign.

The Ascendants of Gemini in 2024 - A Year of Success

For the ascendants of Gemini, 2024 holds a promise of numerous achievements. With Jupiter gracing your 11th House, your financial prospects will be robust. Love relationships will deepen, and for those still unmarried, the prospect of matrimony looms on the horizon. Saturn, acting as the master of your destiny, takes up residence in your favorable house, reigniting stalled plans and setting them in motion. Even stuck endeavors will regain momentum, leading to well-deserved success.

Nonetheless, Rahu and Ketu's presence in your tenth and fourth houses may introduce moments of physical weakness. The positioning of the Sun and Mars in your seventh house at the year's outset may bring fluctuations in business and married life. Additionally, the presence of Mercury and Venus in your sixth house early in the year might accelerate expenses. Throughout 2024, it's crucial to prioritize health and financial management.

Gemini Love Horoscope 2024

- A Year of Romantic Flourish

The Gemini Horoscope 2024 foretells a delightful start to love relationships in the coming year. The benevolent influence of Jupiter on your fifth House will infuse your love life with innocence and purity. You'll emerge as a true, honest partner, committed to sustaining the bonds of love. Mutual understanding and coordination will be at an all-time high, with both partners valuing and respecting each other.

The period from August to September stands out as particularly auspicious for love. During this time, you and your partner will revel in the joys of romance, embarking on long-distance journeys and cherishing quality time together. Plans to take your love to the next level, towards marriage, will solidify in 2024. March may demand caution, but the last quarter of the year will fortify your relationship. Maintaining decorum and respect is key to avoiding any misunderstandings. Honesty and decency will strengthen mutual respect and deepen the connection.

February presents an opportunity for a marriage proposal, but it's advisable to be patient as your proposal may face initial rejection. Don't lose heart, as success is on the horizon, likely arriving around August and solidifying in October.

Gemini Career

The Path to Success

Guiding Your Career Journey in 2024

The Gemini Horoscope 2024 offers valuable insights into your career path for the year. It advises Gemini ascendants to steer clear of shortcuts in 2024. While efficiency may tempt you to take quick routes, remember that long-term success lies in hard work. The year begins on a positive note, promising success in your job. Your swift execution of tasks will set you apart and grant you a competitive edge. Promotion prospects loom between the end of March and April.

Come May, your job may lead you to travel to other states or even abroad. Your dedication and increased sensitivity towards your work will prove to be advantageous. The Gemini Career Horoscope 2024 predicts job opportunities between March 7th and March 31st, as well as from September 18th to October 13th. This period favors those contemplating a job switch. Additionally, a departmental change may occur in May. While the year's outset is favorable, maintaining positive relations with senior officers is crucial to avoid potential issues. Those seeking employment might find opportunities in the latter part of the year.

Gemini Education 2024

Navigating the Academic Path

Guidance for Gemini Students in 2024

The Gemini Horoscope 2024 acknowledges that students may encounter initial challenges in the year. The presence of Ketu in your fourth house could introduce distractions in your education. However, Jupiter's grace will empower you to excel academically. Your persistent efforts and hard work will elevate your educational journey, leading to success. Jupiter will enhance your knowledge and wisdom, while Saturn's influence will necessitate diligent work. Post-April, maintaining focus is vital as obstacles may arise.

For students preparing for competitive exams, this year demands intense dedication for success. The competitive exams could prove challenging, making hard work essential. Saturn, governing the eighth and ninth houses, takes residence in the ninth house, favoring higher education. While some hurdles may surface, you will achieve your degrees and complete your education. The Gemini Horoscope 2024 hints at a favorable start to the year if you aspire to study abroad. Furthermore, the months of August and November will bring success on your educational journey.

Gemini Career 2024

Navigating the Professional Path

Steering Your Career in 2024

The Gemini Horoscope 2024 is your compass for the year, guiding you through the intricacies of your professional life. It strongly advises Gemini ascendants to refrain from seeking shortcuts in 2024. While the allure of efficiency may tempt you to cut corners, the long-term path to success lies in unwavering hard work. The year sets off on a promising note, with a surge of success in your current job. Your exceptional efficiency will place you in a favorable position, often outpacing your peers and providing you with a competitive advantage. The period from the end of March to April is ripe with potential for promotions.

As the calendar turns to May, your job may require you to embark on journeys to other states or even foreign lands. Your heightened commitment and sensitivity towards your work will yield significant benefits. According to the Gemini Career Horoscope 2024, windows of opportunity for new job prospects will open between March 7th and March 31st, as well as from September 18th to October 13th. If you are contemplating a job change, these timeframes are particularly auspicious. Additionally, the possibility of transitioning to a different department looms in May. While the year commences on a positive note, maintaining harmonious relations with senior officers is of paramount importance to sidestep potential pitfalls. For job seekers, opportunities may arise in the latter months of the year.

Gemini Education 2024

Nurturing the Scholar Within

Guidance for Gemini Students in 2024

The Gemini Horoscope 2024 acknowledges that students may encounter initial challenges in the year. The presence of Ketu in your fourth house could introduce distractions in your education. However, the grace of Jupiter will empower you to excel academically. Your persistent efforts and unwavering dedication will elevate your educational journey, ultimately leading to success. Jupiter's benevolent influence will enhance your knowledge and wisdom, while Saturn's presence will necessitate diligent work.

Post-April, maintaining unwavering focus becomes imperative, as unforeseen obstacles may surface. For students preparing for competitive exams, this year will demand an unprecedented level of dedication for success. The competitive exams could prove to be particularly challenging, making relentless hard work the cornerstone of your journey. Saturn, governing the eighth and ninth houses, takes residence in the ninth house, creating a favorable environment for higher education. While the journey may be dotted with hurdles, you will ultimately achieve your academic degrees and complete your education.

The Gemini Horoscope 2024 suggests that the year kicks off favorably, especially if you harbor aspirations of studying abroad. Furthermore, the months of August and November hold the promise of success on your academic journey, providing the opportunity for significant milestones and achievements.

Gemini Finance 2024

Navigating Financial Waters

Charting Your Financial Path in 2024

The Gemini Horoscope 2024 brings insights into your financial journey for the year. Thanks to the presence of Jupiter in the eleventh house, with Saturn casting its benevolent aspect on the ninth house, your financial strength is set to rise. Financial worries will be a thing of the past, with a steady flow of income. However, prudent financial management is advised, as a sudden surge in expenses looms on the horizon. These expenses may, at times, seem unnecessary.

The year kicks off with regular expenditures, and you will also allocate funds towards religious and auspicious endeavors when Jupiter enters your twelfth house on May 1, 2024. As the year unfolds, your expenses will continue to mount. While Saturn ensures stability, a cautious approach remains essential. It's advisable to steer clear of financial risks between February and March. However, the period from April to June emerges as the most favorable window for earning and investing. It is during this time that you'll attain financial stability and soundness.

Gemini Family 2024

Nurturing Family Bonds

Guiding Your Family Life in 2024

The Gemini Horoscope 2024 forewarns of challenges in the family realm in 2024. The presence of Ketu in the fourth house and Rahu in the tenth house will exert pressure and stress on your family life. Caring for your parents becomes paramount, as they may encounter health issues. Trust issues may surface, creating disharmony and occasional family disputes. Open communication and counsel will be vital in averting these challenges.

The period from April to August promises an upswing in family harmony, with everyone living in sync. However, September may introduce property disputes, escalating family stress. Your relationship with siblings will remain positive, with their support extending to your business endeavors. Prioritizing your relationship with siblings and heeding their advice will prove beneficial. On April 23, when Mars transits your tenth house, special attention to your mother's health is imperative. While affection will be shared, small conflicts may arise during this period.

Gemini Health 2024

Nurturing Well-being

Caring for Your Health in 2024

The Gemini Horoscope 2024 sheds light on your health and well-being in the upcoming year. It emphasizes the importance of self-care and vigilance in maintaining good health.

In 2024, your health will largely be stable and robust. The presence of Saturn in your ninth house will contribute to this stability. However, it is essential to maintain a balanced and healthy lifestyle to preserve this well-being.

As the year progresses, it's important to keep an eye on your physical and mental health. Regular exercise, a nutritious diet, and adequate rest are key components of a healthy lifestyle. Pay attention to your stress levels and incorporate stress management techniques into your daily routine.

Additionally, consider regular health check-ups to detect and address any potential health issues early. Your health may require extra attention during Mars' transit in your tenth house on April 23. While this period may introduce minor health concerns, prompt attention and care can mitigate any potential problems.

Overall, 2024 offers the opportunity for good health and well-being, provided you remain proactive in your self-care and health management.

Gemini Love 2024

Nurturing Love and Relationships

Guidance for Your Love Life in 2024

The Gemini Horoscope 2024 delves into the realm of love and relationships, providing valuable insights for the year ahead.

For Gemini natives, 2024 holds the promise of a flourishing love life. The influence of Jupiter on your fifth House infuses your relationships with purity and innocence. This year, you'll embody the essence of a true and honest partner, dedicated to nurturing and sustaining your relationship. The spirit of mutual understanding and coordination will be at its peak, with both partners valuing and respecting each other.

The period between August and September stands as a testament to the flourishing of love in your life. During these months, you and your partner will experience the joys of romance, embarking on memorable journeys together and cherishing quality time. Your commitment will solidify, leading to thoughts of taking your relationship to the next level, including the possibility of marriage.

While the majority of the year flows smoothly, it's essential to maintain decorum and respect, particularly in March. The last quarter of the year will consolidate your relationship and strengthen your bond. Demonstrating decency and honesty will enhance mutual respect and deepen the connection.

Consider proposing marriage to your partner in February; however, be prepared for the possibility of an initial rejection. Patience is key, as success is more likely to come into view around August, with October representing a promising period for your love life.

Gemini Summary

Embracing Life's Journey

The Gemini Horoscope 2024 ushers in a year of opportunities and challenges across various facets of life. Financial stability, robust health, thriving relationships, and educational pursuits await. While challenges may emerge, your adaptability and determination will be your greatest assets in navigating the journey of 2024. Remember to seize opportunities, maintain a healthy balance in life, and prioritize open communication and understanding in your relationships. The year is brimming with potential, and your choices will shape your destiny.

Gemini Child 2024

Nurturing Your Child's Journey

Guidance for Gemini Parents in 2024

The Gemini Horoscope 2024 extends its insights to your role as a parent, shedding light on your child's journey throughout the year.

For those wishing to have a child, the initial half of 2024 holds promise. From January to the end of April, favorable conditions align, increasing the likelihood of a blessed addition to your family. Your child, born during this period, is destined to exhibit obedience and scholarly traits.

Parents who are already blessed with a child will also experience a positive start to the year. Witnessing your child's progress will fill you with joy. However, the period from March 15th to April 23rd, when Mars enters Aquarius, may introduce fluctuations in your child's education and health. Subsequently, from April 23rd to June 1st, health concerns may surface, necessitating your special care and attention.

According to the Gemini Horoscope 2024, the duration from June 1st to July 12th may see an increase in your child's temper. As a parent, it's essential to guide and support them during this phase, steering them away from negative paths in life. Beyond this challenging period, the outlook becomes more favorable, and your child will excel and progress in various aspects of their life.

Gemini Marriage 2024

Nurturing Matrimonial Bonds

Guidance for Your Marriage in 2024

The Gemini Horoscope 2024 explores the dynamics of your marriage in the coming year. The year kicks off with promising prospects for Gemini natives, with the potential for weddings in the early months. Jupiter's grace and favorable marriage conditions contribute to this positive outlook.

For those already married, the beginning of the year may present some challenges. Mars and the Sun will reside in the seventh house of your birth chart, contributing to occasional discord and disputes. Although Jupiter's influence in the seventh house may mitigate these issues, the combined effects of the Sun and Mars may lead to a degree of volatility. Additionally, your life partner's health may experience fluctuations, necessitating your care and attention.

The Gemini Horoscope 2024 offers guidance on maintaining a harmonious relationship with your in-laws and practicing good behavior. Avoiding conflict and disagreements is crucial. As the year progresses, the situation will improve, allowing you and your life partner to understand the significance of mutual participation in a married life. Collaboratively, you will fulfill family responsibilities and nurture your child.

From August to October, you'll find ample opportunities for shared journeys, which may include trips or pilgrimages. These experiences will rejuvenate your energies and provide quality time together, potentially alleviating any tensions. A happy married life awaits, and you can consider making thoughtful gestures, such as purchasing significant gifts or items for your life partner, to further strengthen your bond.

Gemini Sibling 2024

Strengthening Sibling Bonds

Guidance for Your Relationship with Siblings in 2024

The Gemini Horoscope 2024 provides insights into your relationship with your siblings in the upcoming year, offering guidance on nurturing these bonds.

For Gemini natives, the year 2024 is poised to enhance your connection with your siblings. This year, you will prioritize your relationship with your siblings and exhibit obedience and support towards them. This sibling dynamic will prove beneficial to you, contributing to your personal and professional growth.

While maintaining harmonious relations with your siblings, you'll benefit from their guidance and cooperation, particularly in your business endeavors. This mutual support and respect will lay the foundation for a strengthened bond, further enriching your familial relationships.

Gemini Travel 2024

Exploring New Horizons

Embracing Travel Adventures in 2024

The Gemini Horoscope 2024 ushers in a year of travel opportunities and explorations. It encourages you to seize the chance to broaden your horizons and embark on exciting journeys.

Between August and October, multiple occasions will arise for both you and your life partner to embark on trips. These travels may include leisurely trips or even pilgrimages. The experiences will not only rejuvenate your energies but also provide valuable quality time together. It's an ideal time to remove any accumulated tensions and foster a deeper connection.

Gemini Gifting 2024

Nurturing Relationships through Thoughtful Gifts

Guidance on Gift-Giving in 2024

The Gemini Horoscope 2024 advises on the significance of gift-giving in strengthening relationships. It suggests considering meaningful and beneficial gifts for your life partner.

In 2024, keeping in mind your life partner's needs, you have the opportunity to purchase a substantial gift or item that will hold great value for them. Thoughtful gestures through gift-giving will further enhance your marital bond and nurture your relationship.

Gemini Business 2024

Navigating the Business Landscape

Guidance for Your Business Ventures in 2024

The Gemini Horoscope 2024 offers insights and guidance to navigate the business landscape in the upcoming year.

The year's commencement for your business endeavors may be characterized as average. It's crucial to approach the year with caution, given the potential ups and downs in your business trajectory, influenced by the positions of the Sun, Mars, Mercury, and Venus. Maintaining amicable relations with your business partner is essential, as conflicts could have detrimental effects on your business.

The period from January to March requires careful and strategic action, as you will encounter various challenges that demand your attention. However, come April, you'll notice a gradual improvement as the obstacles begin to subside. The movement of the lord of the seventh house to the eleventh house at the year's outset signifies potential profits in your business.

On May 1st, Jupiter will transit to the twelfth house, indicating opportunities for expanding your business through foreign contacts. Foreign travel related to your business is also on the horizon. The period between March 31st and April 24th is particularly auspicious, presenting a significant opportunity that could bring prosperity to your business.

However, exercise caution between October 13th and November 7th, as you may face potential legal proceedings. December is poised to be a successful month for your business.

Gemini Property and Vehicle 2024

Property and Vehicle Considerations

Guidance for Property and Vehicle Decisions in 2024

In the realm of property and vehicle decisions, the Gemini Horoscope 2024 offers guidance to ensure informed choices.

When considering the purchase of a vehicle, exercise caution and make your decision carefully. The presence of Ketu in the fourth house indicates the need for prudence. Choose an auspicious moment for the purchase, as there is a possibility of vehicle damage or accidents due to the influence of Rahu and Ketu. Favorable periods for vehicle purchase include the time when the lord of the fourth house and your zodiac sign, Mercury, is in the ninth house from February 20th to

March 7th and from June 14th to June 29th.

For property-related decisions, there are opportunities to sell property in 2024. Consider the periods from March 26th to April 9th, July 19th to August 22nd, and August 22nd to September 4th as auspicious for property sales. If you're contemplating the acquisition of new property, favorable time frames for purchasing property fall between February 20th and March 7th, March 26th to April 9th, and September 23rd to October 29th.

Gemini Legal Matters 2024

Navigating Legal Affairs

Guidance for Legal Affairs in 2024

The Gemini Horoscope 2024 provides insights and guidance for navigating legal matters in the upcoming year.

Exercise caution between October 13th and November 7th, as this period may involve legal proceedings. It's important to avoid any wrongdoing during this time to prevent legal complications.

Gemini Wealth and Profit

Managing Finances and Gains

Guidance for Your Financial Prosperity in 2024

The Gemini Horoscope 2024 provides insights and guidance to manage your finances and navigate the journey of wealth and profit in the upcoming year.

The start of the year may be characterized as average regarding your financial situation and gains. Expenses will increase, partly due to health concerns and other issues related to the presence of Mercury and Venus in the sixth house. The months of February and March will bring added stress, with Mars in the eighth house and Mercury and Venus moving to the seventh house.

However, the latter half of the year, particularly the third and fourth quarters, will bring more favorable financial prospects. The transit of Jupiter to the twelfth house will influence your earnings and result in increased expenses.

In 2024, there are opportunities to uncover hidden assets, notably due to Mars' presence in the eighth house from February 5th to March 15th. You may also receive ancestral property during this period. It's essential to exercise caution when investing your money, as impulsive decisions can lead to losses.

Special conditions will present themselves for financial gains, primarily between March 7th to April 24th and June 1st to July 12th. This time frame is conducive for such endeavors. The presence of the Sun in your eleventh house from April to May will contribute to financial gains and profits from the government sector.

In summary, it's crucial to exercise caution in lending and receiving money in 2024. While there are opportunities for financial gains, there is also the possibility of financial losses. Wise money management and the habit of saving a portion of your income each month will contribute to your mental and financial well-being.

Lucky Number for Gemini Zodiac Sign in 2024

Guiding Numerical Energies

For the Gemini Zodiac Sign in 2024, the ruling planet, Mercury, bestows luck through the numbers 3 and 6. In astrology, the sum of the year 2024 results in the number 8.

The year 2024 may appear somewhat less favorable for Gemini natives compared to the preceding year, 2023. Success will require heightened effort and more self-reliance. While accomplishments are still within reach, they may come after dedicated and rigorous work. Paying special attention to your health is essential during this period.

If you have any more questions or require additional information, please feel free to ask, and I'll be happy to assist you further.

Frequently Asked Questions about Gemini

1. **How will 2024 unfold for Geminis?**

• The year 2024 is expected to bring a moderate outlook for Geminis.

2. **When can Geminis anticipate a boost in their fortunes during 2024?**

• Geminis can look forward to a promising start to the year, with favorable energies extending until April 30, 2024.

3. **What lies ahead in the destiny of Gemini natives for 2024?**

• In 2024, Geminis are poised to gain recognition, respect, and attain higher positions.

4. **Who are the potential life partners for those born under the Gemini sign?**

• Aquarius and Libra natives are often seen as compatible life partners for Geminis.

5. **Which zodiac signs are most likely to form love connections with Geminis?**

• Geminis tend to share harmonious love relationships with Libra and Aquarius individuals.

Summary for Gemini - January 2024:

Career Emphasis:

- **Opportunities Ahead:** Geminis, your career path is illuminated in January. The month brings promising prospects for those willing to take bold steps. Whether it's considering a new career direction or aiming for a higher position, the stars align in your favor.

- **Analytical Abilities:** Your analytical prowess receives a boost under the influence of the Sun. This means it's an excellent time to make strategic and well-thought-out decisions. Take advantage of this clarity to navigate career choices with confidence.

Family and Relationships:

- **Harmony at Home:** Family matters take precedence this month. The cosmos encourages you to address any lingering differences within your family, fostering a harmonious and supportive home environment.

- **Sentimental Connections:** The Wolf Full Moon adds a touch of sentimentality to your relationships. Embrace this emotional energy, as connections formed during this period may hold special significance, possibly leading to meaningful commitments like marriage.

Career Development and Travel:

- **Advancement Opportunities:**
  The early days of January present a window of opportunity for career advancement. Don't shy away from climbing the career ladder or exploring new job prospects. Your efforts now promise fruitful results.

- **Favorable Travel:** Venus in Sagittarius creates favorable conditions for travel. Consider exploring new horizons, as journeys during this time may provide enriching experiences and broaden your perspective.

Practical Approach:

- **Organized Thinking:** Mercury in Capricorn emphasizes practicality. This influence aids you in organizing scattered thoughts and abstract ideas into a cohesive plan. Use this structured mindset to tackle tasks with efficiency.

- **Guidance for Confidence:** If you're seeking additional confidence in your career path, consider consulting with a coach. A personalized development plan can provide clarity and assurance, enhancing your belief in future successes.

End of the Month Focus:

- **Shift to Everyday Matters:** As January winds down, the pace slows, directing your focus to everyday issues. It's time to transition from holiday festivities to practical concerns. Take this opportunity to get organized and set a productive tone for the coming months.

- **Renewed Willpower:** Mars in Capricorn grants you increased strength and willpower. Leverage this energy to overcome challenges, especially in areas that may have seemed daunting in the past.

- **Embrace the Future:** The January horoscope advises clearing away the remnants of the holiday season. Embrace the future with renewed vigor and a clear space for new opportunities and accomplishments.

February 2024 Horoscope: Gemini Energies

Stability and Reflection:

- Steady Developments: February brings a sense of stability for Geminis. Events unfold slowly and predictably, providing a wide margin for maneuver. Take this time to thoughtfully consider your nearest plans, making adjustments as needed.

- Harmonious Sun in Aquarius: The harmonious influence of the Sun in Aquarius encourages Geminis to reconsider their views on life. Earth signs, usually rational and restrained, can discover new facets of themselves. Changes in appearance or residence will be well-received by others.

- Snow Full Moon: A crucial moment in February is the Snow Full Moon, offering energy that can alter the course of events. Seize this opportunity to reach agreements within the family, emphasizing the importance of compromise.

Early February: Quality Time with Loved Ones:

- Time Management: Competent planning allows Geminis to spend quality time with loved ones in early February. The horoscope emphasizes the need for serious work on relationships, urging against pushing family matters into the background.

- Venus in Capricorn: With Venus in Capricorn heightening leadership ambitions, caution is advised. The desire for victory at any cost may lead to conflicts. Channeling energy into creativity provides a healthier outlet.

Mid-February Motivation:

- Spring Excitement: Mid-February brings abundant motivation, fueled by the anticipation of spring. The general horoscope encourages Geminis to follow their desires and explore new directions. Mercury in Aquarius fosters a feeling of freedom, removing strict limitations.

- Decisive Action: To avoid carrying the burden of old problems, close existing debts, and seek forgiveness from those who may hold a grudge. The time is ripe for decisive action, and possibilities expand limitlessly.

Late February Finances and Enjoyment:

- Stable Financial Situation: The last days of February promise a stable financial situation for Geminis. Extra money may come in, possibly through an increase in salary or a substantial bonus, a sign of favor from superiors.

- Family Focus: Home and family take precedence, according to the February horoscope. It's advised to plan purchases together with loved ones to avoid undermining the budget with spontaneous spending.

- Mars in Aquarius: Daredevils are favored as Mars in Aquarius supports bold actions. Geminis, despite the perplexity of those around them, can revel in success and enjoy life's pleasures. Noisy parties and spontaneous trips are encouraged, embracing the favor of fate.

March 2024 Horoscope: Gemini Energies

Premonition of Love:

- **Spring of Romance:** March brings a premonition of love for Geminis. The first month of spring is marked by a surge of interest from the opposite sex, accompanied by an abundance of compliments. Chance encounters may blossom into beautiful stories.

- **Facing Fears:** The Sun in Pisces brings attention to internal contradictions, requiring Geminis to confront their fears. Long-term planning becomes crucial for success, allowing a calm and methodical pursuit of goals.

Personal Development and Worm Full Moon:

- **Unleashing Potential:** The Worm Full Moon in March becomes a pivotal moment for personal development. It's an opportune time to identify obstacles hindering self-realization, potentially prompting a change in the circle of friends and outlook on life.

- **Learning is Light:** The events in the first days of March underscore the importance of continuous learning. Insufficient professionalism may affect labor productivity, urging Geminis to prioritize quality over quantity.

Seeking training courses is advised to fill knowledge gaps.

- **Optimism and Love of Life:** Venus in Aquarius brings optimism and a love for life. This positive energy helps navigate challenging situations, while mindfulness meditation and other methods contribute to personal development and resilience.

Financial Considerations:

- **Ambiguous Financial Period:** The middle of March presents an ambiguous financial period for Geminis. While there's a stable income, unplanned expenses arise. The general horoscope suggests tuning in to savings and making mindful spending choices for long-term benefits.

- **Mercury in Aries Influence:** Mercury in Aries drives impulsive actions. A wild idea, such as continuing studies abroad, may surface. While it holds promise, Geminis are encouraged to consider more affordable alternatives and weigh the potential dividends.

Calm End of March:

- **Atmosphere of Goodwill:** The calm end of March signals smooth sailing. There's an atmosphere of goodwill in the team, and complete mutual understanding prevails in the family.

- **Opportunities for Strengthening:** The March horoscope foresees opportunities to strengthen positions. Professionalism shines at work, and increased authority within the family is likely. Mars in Pisces elevates thoughts, prompting even down-to-earth individuals to aim high.

- **Bright Impulses and Good Deeds:** Geminis are encouraged not to extinguish bright impulses. Turning this energy into good deeds can lead to transformative life experiences. Earth signs may find fulfillment in joining the volunteer movement, signaling the beginning of a meaningful journey.

April 2024 Horoscope: Gemini Energies

A Busy and Promising Period:

- **Spring Awakening:** April 2024 promises a busy period for Geminis. Spring awakens a craving for new achievements, offering breathtaking possibilities in career changes, financial success, and new acquaintances.

- **Positive Sun in Aries:** The positive influence of the Sun in Aries provides Water signs, including Geminis, with a powerful supply of energy. This energy is advantageous when directed toward the implementation of career goals, fostering confidence and ensuring inevitable success.

- **Jealousy in Personal Life:** In personal life, be cautious about quarrels fueled by jealousy. The crisis may peak during the Pink Full Moon in April. Reconciliation is best achieved through romantic gestures, such as a dinner with a sequel.

Beginning of April - Opportunities and Networking:

- **Cooperation Opportunities:** The beginning of April brings new opportunities for cooperation, with meetings with promising partners on the horizon. Effective communication and upgrading networking skills will contribute to making a positive impression.

- **Charm and Self-Confidence:** Under the influence of Venus in Aries, charm and self-confidence increase, attracting admirers. However, be mindful of potential jealousy-related quarrels in personal relationships. Avoid giving reasons for suspicion, even in innocent interactions.

Mid-April - Self-Expression and Travel:

- **Expressing Yourself:** The middle of April provides an opportunity for self-expression, with new people impacting your life. Travel may be in the cards, and the general horoscope suggests success, particularly due to new acquaintances.

- **Mercury in Aries Influence:** Impulse-driven actions, spurred by Mercury in Aries, may lead to wild ideas, such as continuing studies abroad. While promising, consider more affordable alternatives for education.

Positive End of April - Embracing Change:

- **Spring Mood:** The positive end of April aligns with the spring mood. The horoscope encourages Geminis to embrace change, discard dull clothes, and think and dress in a new, vibrant way.

- **Sailing on Sincerity:** With Mars in Pisces fostering high thoughts, even down-to-earth individuals gain wings. Embrace bright impulses and turn this energy into good deeds. Earth signs can explore new capacities by joining the volunteer movement, signaling the beginning of a transformative journey.

May 2024 Horoscope: Gemini Energies

Caution in Decision-Making:

- **Warning Against Hastiness:** The May 2024 horoscope advises against hasty decisions for Geminis. Impulsive actions can lead to conflicts, disputes, and financial losses. Acting confidently but considering circumstances is key.

- **Sun in Taurus Influence:** The Sun in Taurus enhances qualities like perseverance and diligence. Earth signs, including Geminis, are in a winning position. Success requires developing the right strategy, starting with strengthening the material base.

Flower Full Moon and Family Connection:

- **Significant Family Event:** The Flower Full Moon in May marks a significant event in family life for Geminis. A special connection is established between spouses, enhancing sexual attraction. It's an opportune time to take relationships to a new level by addressing and closing problematic issues.

Financial Stability and Pleasurable Surroundings:

- **Positive Financial Scenario:** The first days of May bring a positive financial scenario for Geminis. Expenses will not exceed income, ensuring a good amount on hand. The horoscope promises a period of stability, allowing for enjoyable expenditures without damaging the budget.

- **Venus in Taurus Influence:** With Venus in Taurus, the ability to feel beauty enhances. The world sparkles with bright colors, and a desire to surround oneself with interesting people and pleasant things arises. Creative atmospheres can birth original ideas, supported by like-minded individuals. Consider renovations in your apartment or personal image.

Increased Self-Confidence and Professional Caution:

- **Mid-May Confidence Boost:** By the middle of May, Geminis experience increased self-confidence and courage. While this positively influences the professional sphere, caution against excessive activity is advised. Calculating each step and setting clear, achievable goals is crucial.

- **Mercury in Aries Influence:** Under Mercury in Aries, impulsive actions may lead to wild ideas, such as continuing studies abroad. While the idea has merit, Geminis should consider more affordable alternatives.

End of May Challenges and Opportunities:

- **Strengthening Control:** The end of May presents temptations, requiring self-control for Geminis. The idea of escaping troubles may arise, but avoidance can worsen problems. The horoscope warns against viewing situations through rose-colored glasses and encourages detailed reconnaissance before making permanent decisions.

- **Mars in Aries Support:** In moments of despair, Mars in Aries acts as a motor generating energy. This energy can be channeled to take a tough, principled position. Water signs, including Geminis, can assert their rights through legal proceedings, emphasizing the need for a cool-headed approach without unnecessary fanaticism.

June 2024 Horoscope: Gemini Energies

Storm of Passions and Personal Life:

- **Summer's Bright Events:** According to the June 2024 horoscope, Geminis can expect a storm of passions as summer begins. Bright events in personal life, including fateful encounters or reunions with first loves, promise a passionate novel and unforgettable experiences.

- **Unruly Sun in Gemini:** The unruly Sun in Gemini brings sharp mood changes, but Geminis, especially Fire signs, possess the intelligence to overcome these fluctuations. Meditative practices are recommended to calm the flow of energy and direct it positively.

- **Clarity in Business during Strawberry Full Moon:** The Strawberry Full Moon in June brings clarity in business, opening the path to new heights. Barriers gradually fade, and stalled projects gain momentum. Career success leads to prosperity.

Stability in Family Life and Communication:

- **Stability in Early June:** Family life in early June brings stability, requiring efforts to maintain. Routine may seem daunting, but finding positives in daily tasks can make them exciting. Venus in Gemini enhances communication effectiveness, fostering mutual understanding.

- **Craving for Communication and Caution:** A strong craving for communication may lead to promiscuity in acquaintances. The horoscope advises directing talents toward positive endeavors, such as organizing charity events, rather than falling into bad company.

Health and Well-being in Mid-June:

- **Health Concerns:** The middle of June sees a decline in health due to accumulated fatigue, with energy levels nearing zero. The general horoscope suggests preventive measures, including giving up alcohol and fast food. Mercury in Gemini brings liveliness and moments of joy.

- **Diversifying Life:** With Mercury's influence, Geminis can immerse themselves in various pursuits, such as the fashion industry, language learning, or upgrading professional skills. Orienting oneself correctly amidst abundant information is crucial.

Financial Calmness at the End of June:

- **Calm Financial Period:** The end of June offers financial calmness, with the possibility of avoiding unexpected expenses. Modest profits combined with the absence of unnecessary expenses help Geminis stay afloat.

- **Mars in Taurus Influence:** Mars in Taurus brings a combination of belligerence and pragmatism, making individuals, including impulsive Fire signs, more practical. The June horoscope encourages redirecting energy for personal and collective benefit, emphasizing the power of goodness.

July 2024 Horoscope: Gemini Energies

Breath of Change and Planned Progress:

- **Progress in Life:** The July 2024 horoscope brings a breath of change, with planned progress leading to the discovery of the right people and necessary resources. While outlines of future successes emerge, it's essential not to rush to conclusions.

- **Atmosphere of Reflection:** The Cancerian atmosphere encourages reflection and a focus on important aspects of life. A deeper sense of belonging to the family prompts individuals to spend more time with loved ones, offering a chance to resolve old conflicts.

Health Concerns and Thunder Full Moon:

- **Well-being:** Health-wise, there's no need to complain about well-being. However, during the Thunder Full Moon in July, the risk of injury increases. Caution is advised, especially while driving and participating in sports. Consider replacing intense training with meditation.

Financial Situation in Early July:

- **Confusing Situation:** The first days of July may seem confusing, but appearances can be deceptive. While there might be enough money for indulgences, challenges arise during the implementation stage. The horoscope cautions against haste and squandering, emphasizing the need for thoughtful action.

- **Venus in Cancer Influence:** Venus in Cancer may trigger inner fears and discomfort. Avoid dwelling on negativity and adopt a more positive outlook. Meditative practices, evening walks, and connecting with like-minded people contribute to achieving harmony.

Soft Control and Positive Direction in Mid-July:

- **Spirit of Adventurism:** By mid-July, life slows down, but the spirit of adventurism persists. While some areas may naturally progress, exercising soft control is advisable. The general horoscope suggests directing energy positively, with air signs finding joy in travel, sports, and hobbies.

- **Mercury in Leo's Influence:** Mercury in Leo enhances the perception of life, infusing each day with special meaning. Trust and the fulfillment of desires become attainable, fostering relations built on respect and mutual assistance.

Summer Mood at the End of July:

- **Captivating Summer Mood:** The end of July brings a captivating summer mood, encouraging individuals to take a break, relax, and enjoy life. The horoscope predicts exciting trips and unforgettable experiences, emphasizing the importance of stocking up on a sunny mood for the future.

- **Health Risks with Mars in Gemini:** With Mars in Gemini, there's a heightened risk of injury, especially due to increased activity. Fire signs, in their impatience and readiness for risks, should be cautious. While extreme sports may not be suitable, light fitness remains a viable option.

August 2024 Horoscope: Gemini Energies

Reducing Activity and Emotional Passions:

- **Reduced Activity in the Last Summer Month:** The August 2024 horoscope advises Geminis to reduce activity as the last summer month unfolds. Life follows the usual script, offering a period of rest for some and temporary calm for others, akin to the calm before the storm.

- **Inflamed Sexual Appetite with Sun in Leo:** In personal life, the Sun in Leo sparks a heightened sexual appetite, leading to serious passions. Air signs, familiar with a range of emotions, from despair to delight, are particularly favored. The Sturgeon Full Moon in August brings inspiration, fostering an interest in the future.

Building a stock of positive emotions is essential.

Calm Start in Early August:

- **Slight Slowdown in Early August:** The pace of life slows down slightly in early August. Embrace the lull, focusing on personal well-being through beauty treatments, sports, shopping, and hobbies. Venus in Virgo streamlines life, facilitating the completion of long-awaited tasks. Perseverance yields positive outcomes, encouraging new and beneficial experiences.

- **Opportunity for Self-Improvement:** Clearing clutter, rekindling relationships, and prioritizing health become achievable with a drop of perseverance. The period offers an opportunity for self-improvement and the realization of long-held dreams.

Return to Routine by Mid-August:

- **Return to Usual Track:** Life returns to its usual track by mid-August, marking the end of the brief period of calm. Abundant communication and the emergence of new faces create opportunities for dating and career development.

- **Initiating Connections and Career Growth:** Taking the initiative in dating and making powerful connections for career growth is encouraged. Mercury in Leo infuses life with meaning, fostering trust, and facilitating the realization of desires. Relationships built on respect and mutual assistance are highlighted.

Career Ambitions and New Prospects at the End of August:

- **Relevance of Career at the End of August:** The topic of career becomes more relevant at the end of August, with ambitions skyrocketing. New prospects and opportunities arise, emphasizing the importance of seizing chances.

- **Possibility of Accidents and Success Away from Home:** Various accidents and unexpected turns are likely. Success is anticipated away from home, requiring readiness to embark on journeys. Mars in Gemini maintains a risk of injury, especially for the impatient Fire signs. Light fitness is recommended over extreme sports.

September 2024 Horoscope: Gemini Energies

Gaining Momentum in Life:

- **Hard Work for Career Heights:** According to the September 2024 horoscope, life is gaining momentum, urging Geminis to work hard for career advancements and financial improvement. Decisive actions, without delay, are key to success during this period.

- **Influence of the Critical Sun in Virgo:** The influence of the Sun in Virgo changes attitudes toward life, heightening criticality. Recognizing and addressing shortcomings becomes essential, offering an opportunity to set goals for overcoming bad habits.

Harvest Full Moon in September:

- **Harvest Full Moon Impact on Personal Life:** The Harvest Full Moon in September brings vibrant colors to personal life. Random relationships are a thing of the past as family values take the spotlight. Overcoming relationship crises for spouses and finding happiness for single individuals are highlighted.

Non-Standard Actions in Early September:

- **Non-Standard Actions Required:** Early September events require non-standard actions, presenting challenges and tests of strength. The horoscope advises sticking to the planned course, as luck may come from unexpected sources. A patron may emerge, or good fortune may favor those who deserve it.

- **Influence of Venus in Libra:** Troubles are experienced less painfully due to the influence of

Venus in Libra. Intuitive understanding guides actions, emphasizing the importance of working on appearance along with communication skills.

Mood Swings and Increased Momentum in Mid-September:

- **Mood Swings Indicate Nature Changes:** Mood swings in mid-September indicate impending changes in nature. The period of rest and carefree entertainment draws to a close, signaling the need to increase momentum.

- **Travel as a Way to Come to Terms with Reality:** The general horoscope for September 2024 suggests that coming to terms with reality is best achieved through travel. Capture a piece of summer and address responsibilities simultaneously. Mercury in Virgo accelerates processes, guiding the right moments for decision-making.

Financial Stability in Late September:

- **Stable Income and Financial Control:** In the last days of September, financial stability prevails as income exceeds expenses. The horoscope predicts stable income, aided by contacts and an impeccable reputation. Opportunities for profitable part-time work or organizing a business may arise.

- **Dealing with Pessimism and Increased Anxiety:** With Mars in Cancer increasing pessimism, some may feel as if the ground is slipping away. Water signs, especially those with increased anxiety, may feel particularly affected. Keeping a sachet of lavender on the desk is advisable for emotional support.

October 2024 Horoscope: Gemini Energies

A Streak of Luck and Personal Life Changes:

- The October 2024 horoscope promises a streak of luck, with changes primarily in personal life. Lonely Geminis have the opportunity to reshape their fate through job or residence changes, leading to new acquaintances.

- The Sun in Libra Calls for Self-Improvement: The position of the Sun in Libra emphasizes the need for self-improvement. Harmony within oneself is essential, prompting Geminis to continuously enhance both internal content and external appearance. Visits to a beautician and nutritionist are recommended.

- Hunter's Full Moon Boosts Concentration of Forces:

Improvement becomes visible after the Hunter's Full Moon in October, marking a time of heightened force concentration. It's an opportune moment to initiate new projects, start studying, or implement business development plans.

Facing New Challenges in Early October:

- New Challenges and Adaptation: In the first days of October, new challenges require quick learning and adaptation. Consulting senior colleagues for their experience and borrowing best practices is advised. The horoscope suggests seeking guidance from a coach to strengthen the spirit.

- Venus in Scorpio Endows with Charisma: Venus in Scorpio brings forth rabid charisma, even for indecisive individuals. This inspirational attitude gives ideas an extra boost, making it easier to decide on experiments, including fashion transformations.

Financial Challenges and Passionate Personal Life in Mid-October:

- Financial Challenges in the Middle of the Month: From a financial standpoint, the middle of October may pose challenges, with each sign facing its own degree of difficulty. Water signs should beware of potential scams promising instant profits.
- Mercury in Scorpio Brings Passion to Personal Life: Mercury in Scorpio introduces passion and romance to personal life. Timid lovers find the courage to confess their feelings in an original and bold manner. Married couples feel liberated, immersing themselves in sensual pleasures.

Unconditional Triumph in Career by Late October:

- Career Success and Sense of Comradeship: Late October becomes a time of unconditional triumph in career matters. Competitors recede into the shadows, while colleagues demonstrate commendable activity. The October horoscope emphasizes the importance of a sense of comradeship for reaching unprecedented heights through mutual assistance.
- Advice for Dealing with Pessimism: While Mars in Cancer may increase pessimism, especially for those with heightened anxiety, keeping a sachet of lavender on the desk is advised for emotional support.

November 2024 Horoscope: Setting Goals and Facing Challenges

Setting Goals in the Energized Month of Scorpio:

- The November 2024 horoscope urges Geminis to set goals, as this period favors undertakings, offering favorable developments in all spheres of life. Increased energy levels in the month of Scorpio enhance natural qualities.
- Favorable Outlook for Fire Signs: Fire signs are highlighted as favorites of fate during this period, with the potential to achieve planned objectives. Buying a lottery ticket might add an extra touch of luck.
- Beaver Full Moon in November for Confessions: The Beaver Full Moon in November is an ideal time for confessions and open expressions of feelings. This

period promotes liberated and open attitudes, sparking romances that can turn lives upside down.

Financial Concerns in Early November:

- Financial Affairs Leave Room for Concern: Early November may bring financial concerns, potentially due to business partners letting you down or unfavorable developments in the labor market. Temporarily reducing expenses and avoiding unnecessary purchases is advised until the situation improves.
- Venus in Virgo Streamlines Life: The influence of Venus in Virgo makes it easier to finish pending tasks and pursue long-held dreams. Taking charge of personal life, relationships, and health is recommended, with perseverance leading to positive outcomes.

Focus on Positive Communication in Mid-November:

- Importance of Positive Communication: In mid-November, the mood will depend on the environment, highlighting the significance of being among pleasant people, whether colleagues or relatives. The horoscope suggests that luck favors brilliant speakers and skillful interlocutors, emphasizing the impact of words on events.
- Trusting Intuition and Embracing Change: Mercury in Sagittarius intervenes, ensuring a happy future by focusing on essential points. Embracing change, trusting intuition, and moving forward are encouraged. Doubts should be addressed with intuition as a guide.

Challenges in Family Life by Late November:

- Challenges in Family Life: The last days of November present challenges in family life, marked by hard work and the need for extensive study, leading to potential outbreaks of irritability. Sorting out issues is discouraged to avoid worsening the family crisis.

- Beneficial Position of Mars in Scorpio: Mars in Scorpio is considered beneficial, providing the strength to emerge victorious from challenging situations. Troubles contribute to personal growth and character strengthening, particularly for Fire signs with an invigorated desire to conquer the world.

- Strengthening Immune System: As Fire signs aim high, it's advisable to start from lower altitudes, focusing on strengthening the immune system for resilience.

Overview: November 2024 encourages Geminis to set ambitious goals across various life spheres. This period is marked by favorable conditions for success if the right steps are taken. Energized by the Scorpio influence, Geminis are advised to leverage their natural qualities for optimal outcomes. The Beaver Full Moon in November promises a surge of liberated emotions, potentially transforming romances into life-altering experiences.

Financial Affairs: Early November presents challenges in financial affairs. While no dire situations arise, cautiousness is urged as business partners may prove unreliable, and the labor market may present unfavorable conditions. Temporary expense reduction is advised until a positive shift occurs. The influence of Venus in Virgo eases the challenges, facilitating the completion of long-desired tasks and relationship rekindling.

Mid-November Communication and Luck: Mid-November highlights the importance of communication. The horoscope emphasizes the significance of well-chosen words, as even a single phrase can alter the course of events. The intervention of Mercury in Sagittarius ensures a positive future by prioritizing key points. Trusting intuition is encouraged for decisive actions and overcoming doubts.

Family Life Dynamics: The last days of November bring challenges in family life. Intense work and study commitments contribute to heightened irritability. Caution is advised in avoiding conflicts that may unveil unpleasant facts. However, the beneficial position of Mars in Scorpio empowers Geminis to emerge victorious from challenging situations, fostering personal growth.

Fire Signs Triumph: The period concludes with Fire signs displaying heightened ambition and a desire to conquer challenges. Initiating from lower altitudes is recommended to avoid premature burnout. Strengthening the immune system is crucial for sustained success.

In Conclusion: November 2024 prompts Geminis to navigate financial challenges, utilize strategic communication, and navigate family dynamics. Success hinges on resilience, effective communication, and maintaining a balanced approach in various life aspects.

December 2024 Horoscope Summary for Geminis:

Embracing Celebration, Strengthening Relationships, Favorable Finances, and New Year Preparations

Overview: In December 2023, Geminis are greeted with a festive atmosphere, signaling the approach of the New Year. Despite impending challenges related to domestic and work issues, an advent calendar can add a touch of excitement and anticipation. The optimistic influence of the Sun in Sagittarius brings enthusiasm to Water signs, encouraging them to address challenges as opportunities for personal growth.

Personal Life: Early December sees a vibrant personal life, with positive events unfolding. Balancing a busy work schedule, Geminis can find time for meaningful dates, leading to strong and reliable relationships. Venus in Libra contributes to a less painful experience of troubles, fostering intuitive understanding and boundary-setting. Appearance enhancement is highlighted, urging a visit to the beautician.

Financial Outlook: Financial prospects in mid-December are favorable, contingent on personal initiative. Active development in multiple directions promises a rewarding return. The general horoscope predicts increased income, making it an opportune time for New Year shopping and thoughtful gift selection. Mercury in Capricorn emphasizes practicality, offering clarity in scattered thoughts. Seeking guidance from a coach can enhance confidence in future endeavors.

Year-End Completion: The concluding days of December promise swift completion of initiated tasks, allowing Geminis to enter the New Year with a light heart. Perseverance and hard work yield positive outcomes, and a focus on the good and belief in the best is encouraged.

Festive Celebrations: Spending the festive night with loved ones is emphasized for a joyful transition to the new year.

Mars in Sagittarius Warning: Mars in Sagittarius urges restraint to avoid abandoning business and missing lucrative opportunities.

Romantic Exploration for Water Signs: Romantic Water signs are advised to balance their desire for change with a realistic approach, potentially exploring new horizons through language studies.

What Are Geminis Into?

Geminis are known for their diverse interests and curiosity about the world. Here's a closer look at what Geminis are into:

1. Books: Geminis have a natural affinity for reading and often have a deep love for books. They enjoy exploring various genres, from fiction to non-fiction, and are avid readers. Whether it's classic literature, contemporary novels, or informational texts, Geminis appreciate the written word.

2. Music: Geminis have a strong connection to music. They enjoy listening to a wide range of musical genres, and their tastes can be eclectic. Attending concerts, music festivals, or simply playing musical instruments may be some of their musical pursuits. Music allows Geminis to express their emotions and creativity.

3. Writing: Many Geminis have a passion for writing. They may engage in various forms of writing, including blogging, journalism, creative storytelling, or even poetry. Their natural communication skills find an outlet in the written word. Writing allows them to share their thoughts, ideas, and experiences with the world.

4. Travel: Geminis have a deep wanderlust and an inherent curiosity about the world. They enjoy exploring new places and experiencing different cultures. Short trips, both near and far, are a common way for them to satisfy their need for adventure. Traveling allows Geminis to gather new stories and anecdotes to share with others.

5. Socializing: Geminis are social butterflies. They thrive on interacting with a wide circle of friends and acquaintances. Their charm, wit, and conversational skills make them magnetic in social settings. They enjoy attending gatherings, parties, and events where they can engage in lively conversations and meet new people.

6. Art and Creativity: Many Geminis have an artistic and creative side. They may explore various forms of artistic expression, such as painting, drawing, photography, or even acting. Their adaptable nature allows them to try different artistic pursuits and express themselves through creativity.

7. Technology: Geminis are often tech-savvy. They are interested in the latest technological advancements and enjoy experimenting with gadgets and devices. They may keep up with the latest trends in the digital world and have a knack for understanding and using technology to their advantage.

8. **Learning:** Geminis have an insatiable thirst for knowledge. They are perpetual learners who are constantly seeking new information and experiences. They may enroll in courses, workshops, or pursue self-directed learning to expand their horizons. They value education and intellectual growth.

9. **Networking:** Geminis are skilled networkers. They enjoy connecting with people from various backgrounds and professions. Building a diverse network of friends, mentors, colleagues, and acquaintances is important to them. They thrive in environments where they can exchange ideas and knowledge with a wide range of individuals.

10. **Adventure:** Geminis appreciate adventure in various forms. Whether it's embarking on a spontaneous road trip, trying out a new sport, or participating in adrenaline-pumping activities like skydiving or bungee

jumping, they seek excitement and novelty.

11. Communication: Given their natural talent for communication, Geminis enjoy engaging in conversations. They are excellent conversationalists and find fulfillment in sharing their thoughts, ideas, and experiences with others. They appreciate open and engaging dialogues.

12. Learning Languages: Geminis often have an interest in learning different languages. Their linguistic curiosity makes them eager to pick up new languages or improve their language skills. This aligns with their love for communication and interaction.

Overall, Geminis have a wide array of interests, driven by their insatiable curiosity and adaptability. Their versatile nature allows them to explore and engage in various activities, making them well-rounded and fascinating individuals.

Geminis Attractive Traits

Geminis possess a unique set of attractive traits that make them stand out in social and romantic settings. Here are some of the most appealing qualities of Geminis:

1. Charming Conversationalists: Geminis are renowned for their exceptional communication skills. Their ability to engage in witty and captivating conversations makes them highly attractive. They can talk about a wide range of topics, keeping others entertained and intrigued.

2. Adaptable Nature: Geminis are known for their adaptability. They can effortlessly switch between various roles and environments, making them easy to get along with. Their flexibility in different situations is a highly appealing quality.

3. Curious and Inquisitive: Geminis have an insatiable curiosity about the world. Their inquisitive nature often leads to exciting and stimulating discussions. This intellectual curiosity can be highly attractive to those who appreciate deep and meaningful conversations.

4. Quick Learners: Geminis have a knack for learning quickly. Whether it's acquiring new skills, understanding complex concepts, or adapting to new situations, their ability to grasp information rapidly is impressive and appealing.

5. Sense of Humor: Geminis often have a great sense of humor. They enjoy making others laugh and can use humor to break the ice in social interactions. A good laugh shared with a Gemini is both enjoyable and attractive.

6. Social Butterfly: Geminis are naturally sociable and enjoy socializing with a wide circle of friends and acquaintances. Their magnetic presence in social settings and their ability to connect with people is an attractive quality.

7. Youthful Energy: Geminis exude youthful energy and a sense of playfulness. They often maintain a youthful outlook on life, which can be infectious and appealing to those around them.

8. Open-Mindedness: Geminis are open-minded and receptive to new ideas and experiences. Their willingness to embrace different perspectives and explore the unknown is an attractive quality for those who value diversity and open-mindedness.

9. Adventurous Spirit: Geminis are adventurous and willing to try new things. Their enthusiasm for adventure and exploration can inspire others and create exciting opportunities for shared experiences.

10. Optimism: Geminis tend to be optimistic by nature. Their positive outlook on life and their ability to maintain hope and enthusiasm, even in challenging times, is a highly attractive quality.

11. **Eloquence:** Geminis are often eloquent speakers. Their ability to express themselves with clarity and grace is appealing and can make them stand out in both professional and personal situations.

12. **Natural Flirtation:** Geminis are natural flirters, and their playfulness can be charming. While their flirtatious nature is usually lighthearted, it adds an element of intrigue to their interactions.

13. **Versatility:** Geminis are versatile individuals who can adapt to various roles and situations. Their multifaceted nature and ability to embrace change are attractive qualities for those who appreciate versatility.

These attractive traits, combined with their dynamic and engaging personalities, make Geminis captivating and appealing to a wide range of people. Their ability to connect on both intellectual and social levels adds to their charm and desirability.

Who Gets on Best with of Geminis

Geminis are known for their versatile and sociable nature, making them compatible with a wide range of personalities. However, some zodiac signs tend to have particularly harmonious relationships with Geminis due to shared interests, communication styles, and complementary qualities. Here are the zodiac signs that often get along best with Geminis:

1. **Libra (September 23 - October 22):** Libra and Gemini share an Air element, which fosters a strong mental connection. Both signs value communication, balance, and harmony, making their interactions pleasant and intellectually stimulating. They appreciate each other's sociable nature and enjoy engaging in thought-provoking conversations.

8. Leo (July 23 - August 22): Leo's charismatic and outgoing nature complements Gemini's sociable disposition. Both signs enjoy the spotlight and thrive in social settings. They appreciate each other's sense of humor and the ability to make any gathering more entertaining.

9. Sagittarius (November 22 - December 21): Sagittarius and Gemini share a strong sense of curiosity and a love for exploration. They both have a desire for freedom and independence. Their adventuresome spirits align well, and they can embark on exciting journeys together, both mentally and physically.

10. Aries (March 21 - April 19): Aries and Gemini share a mutual love for adventure and excitement. They both enjoy spontaneity and have an energetic, youthful spirit. While Aries provides the drive and leadership, Gemini contributes its communication skills, making this a dynamic and active partnership.

11.   **Leo (July 23 - August 22):** Leo's charismatic and outgoing nature complements Gemini's sociable disposition. Both signs enjoy the spotlight and thrive in social settings. They appreciate each other's sense of humor and the ability to make any gathering more entertaining.

12.   **Sagittarius (November 22 - December 21):** Sagittarius and Gemini share a strong sense of curiosity and a love for exploration. They both have a desire for freedom and independence. Their adventuresome spirits align well, and they can embark on exciting journeys together, both mentally and physically.

While these zodiac signs often have great compatibility with Geminis, it's essential to remember that astrology is just one aspect of a person's personality. Individual differences and unique characteristics play a significant role in any relationship. Ultimately, the success of a relationship depends on the individuals involved and their ability to communicate, understand, and support each other.

Turn-Ons

Geminis are known for their diverse and ever-curious nature, which extends to their turn-ons and attractions. While individual preferences can vary greatly, here are some common turn-ons and factors that tend to arouse Geminis:

1. **Intellectual Stimulation:** Geminis are drawn to partners who can engage them in intellectually stimulating conversations. They find intelligence and wit highly attractive. Engaging in debates, discussing intriguing ideas, or sharing knowledge can be a major turn-on for Geminis.

2. **Variety and Novelty:** Geminis have a thirst for new experiences and variety in life. They are often excited by the prospect of trying new activities, visiting different places, or exploring

uncharted territory. Partners who can introduce novelty into the relationship and surprise them are likely to arouse their interest.

3. Playfulness: Geminis have a playful and youthful spirit. They are attracted to partners who can be lighthearted, humorous, and enjoy playful banter. Laughter and fun interactions can be a significant turn-on for them.

4. Adventurous Spirit: Geminis appreciate partners who share their sense of adventure. They are turned on by the idea of embarking on exciting journeys, both physical and mental. Outdoor adventures, travel, and trying new activities together can be highly stimulating for Geminis.

5. Effective Communication: Geminis value effective communication and honesty in a relationship. Partners who can express themselves clearly and openly are more likely to arouse Geminis. They find it enticing when their partners are good listeners and can engage in deep, meaningful conversations.

6. Spontaneity: Geminis have a spontaneous side, and they are often attracted to partners who can embrace impromptu adventures and unplanned moments. Being open to spontaneity in the bedroom or in everyday life can be a turn-on for Geminis.

7. Curiosity: Geminis are naturally curious and inquisitive. They are intrigued by partners who share their curiosity and a desire to learn and explore. Engaging in joint learning experiences or discussing fascinating topics can be a turn-on.

8. Flirtation: Geminis are known for their flirtatious nature, and they often enjoy flirting with their partners. Playful teasing, compliments, and romantic gestures can ignite their passions.

9. Independence: While Geminis value togetherness, they also appreciate partners who respect their need for independence. A partner who allows them freedom and personal space can be a turn-on, as it aligns with their adaptable and free-spirited nature.

10. Mental Connection: Geminis are sapiosexual to some extent, meaning they are attracted to a person's mind. A strong mental connection, shared interests, and a partner who challenges them intellectually can be highly arousing.

It's important to remember that individual preferences vary, and not all Geminis are attracted to the same things. Effective communication and understanding your partner's specific desires are essential in any relationship. Ultimately, the most significant turn-on for a Gemini is feeling mentally and emotionally connected with their partner.

Turn-Offs

While Geminis have diverse tastes and preferences, there are certain turn-offs and behaviors that can dampen their enthusiasm and attraction. Here are some common turn-offs for Geminis:

1. **Boredom:** Geminis thrive on novelty and intellectual stimulation. Monotonous routines, predictable conversations, and a lack of excitement can quickly turn them off. They prefer partners who keep things interesting and engaging.

2. **Close-Mindedness:** Geminis appreciate open-mindedness and the ability to adapt to different perspectives. Stubbornness, inflexibility, and resistance to new ideas can be major turn-offs for them.

3. **Lack of Communication:** Effective communication is essential for Geminis. Partners who struggle to

express themselves clearly, avoid meaningful conversations, or are poor listeners may frustrate Geminis and diminish their attraction.

4. Rudeness: Geminis value politeness and respectful behavior. Rude or disrespectful actions, impolite language, or offensive comments can be a major turn-off.

5. Overbearing Behavior: Geminis enjoy their freedom and independence. Partners who become overly controlling, possessive, or demanding of their time and attention can trigger feelings of suffocation and turn them off.

6. Negative Vibes: Geminis prefer positive and optimistic interactions. Constant negativity, complaining, and a pessimistic outlook on life can be draining for Geminis and reduce their attraction.

7. Lack of Playfulness: Geminis have a playful and youthful nature. A partner who is overly serious, lacks a sense of humor, or cannot engage in playful banter may not align with their preferences.

8. Insecurity: Geminis appreciate confidence and self-assuredness in their partners. Insecurity, self-doubt, and a constant need for reassurance can be a turn-off, as Geminis prefer partners who are secure in themselves.

9. Being Clingy: Geminis value their personal space and independence. Overly clingy or needy behavior can make them feel trapped and result in diminished attraction.

10. Rigidity: Geminis are adaptable and enjoy trying new things. A partner who is resistant to change, overly structured, and inflexible can be a turn-off, as it clashes with their spontaneous nature.

11. Dishonesty: Honesty is crucial for Geminis. Partners who lie, manipulate, or conceal the truth may erode their trust and attractiveness.

12.   Lack   of   Curiosity:
Geminis are naturally curious and love
learning. A partner who lacks curiosity,
doesn't   engage   in   meaningful
conversations, or shows disinterest in
exploring new topics may not resonate
with them.

**13.   Non-Adventurous
Nature:** Geminis appreciate adventure
and exploration. A partner who is risk-
averse, avoids new experiences, or resists
trying new activities can diminish their
enthusiasm.

It's important to remember that
individual Geminis may have their own
unique turn-offs and preferences.
Effective   communication   and
understanding your partner's specific
dislikes are key to maintaining a
harmonious and fulfilling relationship.

Astrological Remedies

Astrological remedies are practices or actions that individuals can follow based on their astrological signs to improve various aspects of their lives, including health, relationships, career, and overall well-being. While astrology is not a science and should be taken with a grain of salt, some people find value in exploring these remedies for personal growth and self-awareness. Here are some general astrological remedies that Geminis may consider:

1. **Gemstone Therapy:** Gemstones associated with the ruling planet of Gemini, Mercury, include emerald and green agate. Geminis can wear these gemstones as jewelry or keep them in their living spaces to enhance communication, mental clarity, and decision-making.

2. **Color Therapy:** Geminis can incorporate colors associated with their

zodiac sign, such as light green and yellow, into their surroundings. These colors can create a harmonious atmosphere and promote positive energy.

3. Meditation and Mindfulness: To calm their restless minds and enhance their focus, Geminis may benefit from meditation and mindfulness practices. This can help reduce anxiety and improve their decision-making abilities.

4. Yoga and Breathing Exercises: Engaging in yoga and deep breathing exercises can help Geminis manage stress and maintain mental balance. These practices encourage relaxation and inner peace.

5. Mantras and Affirmations: Geminis can create personal mantras or affirmations that resonate with their goals and aspirations. Reciting these daily can boost confidence and motivation.

6. Mental Stimulation: Geminis thrive on intellectual challenges. Engaging in puzzles, brain-teasers, or lifelong learning can keep their minds sharp and active.

7. Journaling: Keeping a journal to document thoughts, ideas, and experiences can help Geminis organize their thoughts and develop self-awareness.

8. Communication Enhancement: Geminis can work on improving their communication skills through public speaking classes, communication workshops, or joining debate clubs.

9. Adaptability Practice: To enhance their adaptability, Geminis can regularly engage in activities that take them out of their comfort zone, such as traveling to new places or trying new hobbies.

10. Networking: Building a strong social network can be beneficial for Geminis' personal and professional growth. Attending social events, networking, and making new friends can expand their horizons.

11. Stress Management: Developing stress management techniques, such as time management, can help Geminis maintain a healthy work-life balance.

12. Mental Health Check: Regularly checking in with a mental health professional can be valuable for Geminis, as it allows them to address any mental health concerns proactively.

It's important to note that astrological remedies are not a substitute for professional advice or medical treatment. Individuals should consult experts in their respective fields for any health or mental health concerns. While some people find astrological remedies to be a source of comfort and personal growth, it's essential to approach astrology with a balanced perspective and use these practices in conjunction with other self-improvement strategies.

Preferred Gifts:

Choosing a thoughtful gift for a Gemini can be a delightful experience, as they appreciate creativity, intellectual stimulation, and social interaction. When selecting a gift for a Gemini, consider items that cater to their diverse interests and vibrant personality. Here are some preferred gift ideas for Geminis:

1. Books: Geminis often have a deep love for reading and learning. Gift them a selection of books by their favorite authors, or explore topics they're passionate about, such as science fiction, self-help, or mysteries.

2. Art Supplies: For the creative Gemini, art supplies like sketchbooks, high-quality pens, or watercolor sets can be a wonderful gift. Encourage their artistic side and help them express their ideas visually.

3. Tech Gadgets: Geminis are typically tech-savvy. Consider gifting them the latest gadgets, such as headphones, smartwatches, or tablet accessories, to keep them connected and entertained.

4. Subscription Services: Sign them up for subscription services that match their interests, whether it's a streaming platform for movies and TV shows, an audiobook service, or a magazine subscription.

5. Board Games and Puzzles: Geminis enjoy games that challenge their minds. Board games, jigsaw puzzles, or brain-teasing puzzles can provide hours of entertainment.

6. Travel Accessories: If your Gemini loves to travel, consider practical travel accessories like luggage, passport holders, or a stylish travel backpack to make their adventures more enjoyable.

7. Unique Jewelry: Surprise them with unique and stylish jewelry pieces, such as personalized necklaces, bracelets, or earrings. Consider gemstone jewelry featuring their birthstone, which is pearl for Geminis.

8. **Writing Tools:** Geminis often appreciate quality writing instruments, such as elegant pens or fountain pens. Pair them with a luxurious journal for them to jot down their thoughts and ideas.

9. **Outdoor Gear:** If your Gemini enjoys outdoor activities, gift them hiking or camping gear, such as a sturdy backpack, a portable hammock, or a set of binoculars for birdwatching.

10. **Classes and Workshops:** Geminis thrive on learning and expanding their knowledge. Enroll them in a class or workshop related to their interests, whether it's cooking, photography, or a foreign language.

11. **Personalized Gifts:** Consider personalized gifts like custom-made artwork, monogrammed

accessories, or a photo book featuring memorable moments you've shared together.

12. Concert or Event Tickets: Geminis love socializing and attending events. Surprise them with tickets to a concert, theater performance, sporting event, or any special occasion they'll enjoy.

13. Gourmet Food and Wine: Treat your Gemini to gourmet food and fine wine. Create a gift basket filled with their favorite treats, chocolates, or a selection of wine and cheese.

14. Fitness Gear: If they're into fitness, consider fitness gear like a yoga mat, fitness tracker, or stylish activewear that complements their active lifestyle.

15. Hobby-Related Gifts: Find out about their hobbies and interests, and choose gifts that align with those passions. Whether it's gardening, cooking, or model building, there are many hobby-related gifts to explore.

Geminis appreciate thoughtful and versatile gifts that cater to their multifaceted nature. Ultimately, the best gift for a Gemini is one that reflects their interests and shows that you've considered their dynamic personality and diverse tastes.

Lucky Stones

Geminis are associated with specific lucky gemstones that are believed to bring them good fortune, protection, and positive energy. These gemstones resonate with the energetic and adaptable nature of Geminis. Here are some lucky stones for Geminis:

1. Agate: Agate is a grounding and stabilizing stone, which can help Geminis stay balanced and focused. It promotes self-acceptance, dispels negativity, and enhances mental clarity.

2. Citrine: Citrine is known as the "merchant's stone" and is associated with wealth, success, and abundance. It encourages positivity, creativity, and mental clarity, making it a perfect match for Geminis.

3. Pearl: Pearl is the traditional birthstone for Geminis. It symbolizes purity, wisdom, and emotional balance. Pearls are said to bring harmony to the wearer's life and enhance their communication skills.

4. Tiger's Eye: Tiger's Eye is a protective stone that helps Geminis stay grounded. It enhances confidence, self-worth, and mental strength. This stone can also provide clarity during decision-making.

5. Aquamarine: Aquamarine is a soothing and calming gemstone. It promotes clear communication and helps Geminis express themselves with ease. It's associated with emotional balance and tranquility.

6. Alexandrite: Alexandrite is a rare and unique gemstone that changes color from green in natural light to red under incandescent light. It symbolizes adaptability and creativity, qualities that resonate with Geminis.

7. Amber: Amber is known for its healing and protective properties. It can help Geminis release negative energy, reduce stress, and boost their vitality.

8. Lapis Lazuli: Lapis Lazuli is a stone of wisdom and truth. It enhances intellectual abilities and helps Geminis in their quest for knowledge and self-expression.

9. Moonstone: Moonstone is associated with emotional balance, intuition, and self-discovery. It can help Geminis connect with their inner emotions and enhance their intuition.

10. Peridot: Peridot is a stone of transformation and personal growth. It encourages self-acceptance and personal development, assisting Geminis in their quest for self-improvement.

Geminis can benefit from wearing or carrying these lucky gemstones to align with their dynamic and communicative nature. Keep in mind that the effectiveness of gemstones is a matter of personal belief, and the true power of these stones lies in the intention and energy that individuals invest in them.

Adversaries to Gemini natives?

- Virgo and Pisces are typically considered the least compatible and potentially **Gemini and Aries Sexual & Intimacy Compatibility (90%):** In the realm of sexual and intimate compatibility, Gemini and Aries bring a potent mix of passion, energy, and curiosity. Their bedroom escapades are characterized by creativity and a disregard for conventional norms. What's particularly advantageous is their mutual indifference to the opinions of others. In its healthier expression, this union is a fusion of ardor, vitality, and a thirst for exploration. However, in less harmonious times, their sexual encounters might be fraught with acerbic exchanges and verbal aggression. Fortunately, both partners possess resilient dispositions and aren't easily wounded, which can make the experience exciting and distinctive for them.

- **Gemini & Aries Trust (40%):**
Trust issues loom as a significant challenge in this relationship. Aries, fueled by passionate impulses and ruled by Mars, is prone to jealousy. In contrast, Gemini, under the governance of Mercury, often exhibits changeable behavior that might erroneously convey untrustworthiness. These trust-related dilemmas can engender arguments and misunderstandings, with the potential for Aries to seek another partner, even while still in the relationship, and Gemini becoming emotionally detached.

- **Gemini & Aries Communication And Intellect (85%):**
The facet of communication and intellectual compatibility can become a source of strength in this union. Gemini excels in the art of conversation, whereas Aries may grapple with it. Gemini can assume the role of a mentor, aiding Aries in refining their conversational skills. Nevertheless, the assertive ego of Aries

may occasionally clash with this dynamic if they perceive Gemini as overly domineering in their communication.

- **Gemini & Aries Emotions (60%):** The emotional dimension is a complex territory for this pairing. Aries carries fervent emotions but finds it challenging to articulate them, while Gemini typically stays near the surface, not being naturally predisposed to intense emotions. When they manage to engage in constructive dialogue, they can establish a groundwork for more meaningful emotional exchanges.

- **Gemini & Aries Values (75%):** When considering values, Aries places a premium on clarity and conciseness, which may diverge from Gemini's proclivity for circumlocution. Gemini values knowledge and rational thought, and Aries might satisfy these criteria to a certain extent, provided they avoid impulsive decision-making.

- **Gemini & Aries Shared Activities (50%):** In shared activities, both signs relish excitement and adventure. Aries radiates energy, while Gemini continually generates innovative ideas, making them enthusiastic participants in diverse and challenging endeavors. They motivate and challenge each other, with neither inclined to turn down an adventurous proposition.

- In summation, the **Gemini and Aries relationship** is often exhilarating and demanding, presenting both partners with opportunities for learning and active engagement. Yet, trust issues and the imperative need for meaningful conversation should be held in consideration. Despite their discrepancies, their shared ardor for adventure frequently binds them together.

Gemini and Aries Overall Compatibility:

Overall, the connection between Gemini and Aries is characterized by a dynamic blend of passion, energy, and exploration. Their shared love for adventure often eclipses many of their conflicts and discrepancies. However, the relationship's success hinges on their ability to address trust issues and engage in meaningful conversations.

Both signs should strive to understand each other better and work on building trust to ensure a harmonious and enduring partnership. With open communication and a willingness to accommodate each other's needs, the Gemini and Aries pairing can lead to a passionate and exhilarating journey together. The challenges they face can be overcome with patience and a commitment to mutual growth and understanding.

As with any relationship, individual variations play a significant role, and the success of the Gemini and Aries connection ultimately depends on the specific individuals involved and their willingness to adapt and grow together.

Gemini and Taurus Relationship Analysis

- **Gemini & Taurus Sexual & Intimacy Compatibility (5%):** Taurus, an Earth sign, craves physical touch and sensual pleasures, while Gemini, an Air sign, prioritizes intellectual stimulation over physical intimacy. This mismatch in desires can lead to challenges in their sex life. Taurus seeks comfort in cuddling and sensual experiences, while Gemini may become disinterested quickly, causing frustration for both partners.

- **Gemini & Taurus Trust (10%):** Trust issues can plague this couple. Gemini's resistance to commitment can trigger Taurus' need for security. This mismatch can lead to jealousy and insecurity on Taurus' part and evasion and distraction from Gemini, creating a cycle of distrust.

- **Gemini & Taurus Communication And Intellect (60%):** Taurus and Gemini have differing intellectual needs. Gemini values mental stimulation and a dynamic exchange of ideas, while Taurus is more grounded and practical. Taurus can provide stability and structure, which Gemini may appreciate, but disagreements may arise when Gemini's constant need for variety clashes with Taurus' desire for routine.

- **Gemini & Taurus Emotions (35%):** Emotional connection is not a strong suit for this couple. Taurus feels deeply but struggles to express their emotions, while Gemini tends to keep emotions at a surface level. Taurus' stable presence can sometimes help Gemini feel safe, but true emotional understanding remains a challenge.

- **Gemini & Taurus Values (1%):** Their values diverge significantly. Taurus values the tangible, material world, and emotional stability, while Gemini values intellectual exploration, adaptability, and change. Finding common ground in their values can be quite difficult.

- **Gemini & Taurus Shared Activities (25%):** Taurus prefers a slower, more deliberate pace in their activities, whereas Gemini seeks novelty and variety. This mismatch can lead to disagreements about how to spend their time together. Finding shared interests may require compromise.

- **In summation,** the relationship between Gemini and Taurus faces considerable challenges. Their differences in sexual needs, trust issues, and contrasting intellectual and emotional preferences can strain the partnership. While there may be moments of connection, their fundamental disparities may pose ongoing difficulties.

Gemini & Gemini: A Mirror of Twins

• **Gemini & Gemini Sexual & Intimacy Compatibility (80%):** Two Geminis in a sexual relationship can be a whirlwind of ideas and exploration. They thrive on learning and teaching in the bedroom, often finding excitement in trying new things. However, sustaining depth in their sexual life may prove challenging.

• **Gemini & Gemini Trust (50%):** Trust may not be a central issue for these two. They understand each other's ever-changing moods and don't mind the lack of predictability. Their freedom-loving natures keep them from expecting long-term commitment.

• **Gemini & Gemini Communication And Intellect (99%):** Communication never ceases in a Gemini-Gemini pairing. They share a common language and are continually engaged in discussions, debates, and chats. Mutual respect and active listening are key to maintaining their intellectual connection.

• **Gemini & Gemini Emotions (70%)**: Geminis aren't known for being highly emotional, and they accept this about each other. Their emotional satisfaction often derives from their intellectual connection, but it can be disrupted if someone else ignites their emotions.

• **Gemini & Gemini Values (99%)**: Freedom is a shared value that both Geminis passionately embrace. They avoid tedious details and obligations, focusing on maintaining their independence. However, beneath their intellectual exterior lies a yearning for intimacy and compassion.

• **Gemini & Gemini Shared Activities (99%)**: They enthusiastically share a wide range of activities, driven by their curiosity and mutual support. Whether it's something they both want to do or a spontaneous adventure, they are inseparable explorers.

- **In Summary**: A relationship between two Geminis is a dynamic and ever-evolving journey. They share an understanding like no other, but their multifaceted personalities can lead to wanderlust in search of depth. If they can discover and nurture their inner cores, their connection can be enduring.

Gemini & Cancer: Balancing Differences

- **Gemini & Cancer Sexual & Intimacy Compatibility (5%)**: Gemini and Cancer have varying desires when it comes to intimacy. Gemini seeks adventure and change, while Cancer craves a deep emotional connection. Finding a middle ground is essential for their sexual satisfaction.

• **Gemini & Cancer Trust (25%)**: Trust may not be a major concern if both partners respect each other's need for freedom. However, Cancer needs to give Gemini space to maintain trust, as Gemini can be reluctant to commit.

• **Gemini & Cancer Communication And Intellect (70%)**: Gemini excels in communication and finds comfort opening up to Cancer. The "motherly" aspect of Cancer nurtures the inner child of Gemini, enhancing their intellectual bond.

• **Gemini & Cancer Emotions (10%)**: Gemini's rational nature can make it challenging to grasp Cancer's emotional needs. Their emotional connection may suffer due to this disconnect. However, Gemini's ability to find emotions in various aspects of life can help bridge the gap.

• **Gemini & Cancer Values (1%)**: Their differing value systems can create conflict, especially in their primary goals for a relationship. Gemini values rationality, while Cancer places significance on emotional connections.

• **Gemini & Cancer Shared Activities (15%)**: Their shared activities depend on Cancer's energy level. While Gemini craves constant change and curiosity, Cancer seeks stability and home life. Finding a balance can be a challenge, but it's crucial for their compatibility.

• **In Summary**: Gemini and Cancer face significant differences in their desires and values. For this relationship to work, both partners need to make adjustments and embrace each other's needs. Balancing freedom and emotional connection is essential for their success.

Gemini & Leo: A Playful Connection

• **Gemini & Leo Sexual & Intimacy Compatibility (90%)**: Gemini and Leo have a strong sexual connection. Gemini's ideas and excitement complement Leo's energy, creativity, and love. Leo can teach Gemini to create a deeper emotional connection, leading to an adventurous and fulfilling sex life.

• **Gemini & Leo Trust (45%)**: Trust can be a challenge due to their different focus on their own needs. Communication and sharing are essential to build trust, preventing issues like dishonesty or infidelity.

• **Gemini & Leo Communication And Intellect (95%)**: Both signs are rational and value intellectual strength. They communicate openly, even if it means being straightforward. Their intellectual bond is strong, and they support each other's opinions, even if they have differences.

• **Gemini & Leo Emotions (85%)**: Leo's warmth and Gemini's charm create wonderful emotions. Their relationship is full of support, respect, and emotional connection. They display their feelings verbally and cherish their love.

• **Gemini & Leo Values (99%)**: Both value intelligence and independence, making them a perfect match. Gemini appreciates Leo's support and inner child, while Leo appreciates Gemini's freedom.

• **Gemini & Leo Shared Activities (80%)**: Gemini's desire for variety in activities complements Leo's willingness to indulge in lavish experiences. While Gemini is always on the move, Leo enjoys moments of relaxation. Their mutual respect for each other's needs allows them to balance their activities.

• **In Summary**: Gemini and Leo share a playful and exciting connection. Their relationship is built on mutual respect, laughter, and a willingness to adjust to each other's needs. They find joy in their shared adventures and create a solid foundation of joyous experiences.

Gemini & Virgo: Intellectual Connection with Challenges

• **Gemini & Virgo Sexual & Intimacy Compatibility (5%)**: Despite both being ruled by Mercury, their sexual connection is challenging. Gemini is explorative, while Virgo is sensitive and shy. Communication is vital, but endless discussions may hinder their intimacy, leaving them distant.

• **Gemini & Virgo Trust (1%)**: Trust can be a significant issue. Gemini's evasiveness and Virgo's trust issues can lead to conflicts and lack of trust. Both must respect and communicate with each other to build security.

• **Gemini & Virgo Communication And Intellect (80%)**: Both signs are ruled by Mercury, and their communication is generally good. However, their approach to intellect differs. They should recognize each other's qualities and let their partner help.

• **Gemini & Virgo Emotions (55%)**: Gemini is not known for being emotional, but they share a unique emotional connection. Virgo has issues with self-worth and fear, which affects their emotions. Both signs need to understand each other's occasional need to be alone or to explore.

- **Gemini & Virgo Values (70%)**: They appreciate intelligence, resourcefulness, and practicality. Their emotional intelligence brings them closer, as they value rationality and practicality in daily life.

- **Gemini & Virgo Shared Activities (30%)**: Their mutable nature makes them change locations and interests frequently. Virgo's hesitation about new experiences and Gemini's wandering tendencies may create challenges in finding activities to share.

- **In Summary**: Gemini and Virgo share an intellectual connection, but their relationship can be unpredictable and changeable. They need to respect each other's differences and not judge each other's intelligence superficially. If they find love, they can become a unique union of Air and Earth Mercury, but it requires understanding and open communication.

Gemini & Libra: A Meeting of Air Signs

Gemini & Libra Sexual & Intimacy Compatibility (80%): Gemini and Libra, both Air signs, share a strong mental connection that extends to their sexual compatibility.

They can freely communicate their desires, which is a significant advantage in the bedroom. Gemini's charm and playfulness can help Libra, who often has a fragile ego, open up and express their emotions during sex. Libra's sensuality complements Gemini's curiosity and willingness to explore new techniques and adventures in the sexual realm.

Their main goal is to find a balance between their emotional needs, and if they manage this, their sex life can be satisfying and dynamic.

Gemini & Libra Trust (95%): Libra's trust is earned through character and honesty. When they choose a partner, they do so after careful consideration and tend to believe in their partner's words and actions. Gemini, in turn, respects Libra's need for social interaction and doesn't find it threatening. This mutual understanding can lead to a high level of trust in their relationship.

Gemini & Libra Communication And Intellect (60%): Gemini is highly opinionated and often speaks their mind. Libra, however, is sensitive to criticism and can take Gemini's comments personally, leading to communication challenges.

Their lack of tolerance for each other's opinions can make their discussions hurtful. Gemini's need to share knowledge and teach can sometimes come across as trying to prove their intellectual dominance, which may upset Libra. To make this relationship work, they must learn to appreciate each other's unique qualities and communicate with more sensitivity.

Gemini & Libra Emotions (90%): Both Gemini and Libra tend to focus on their mental processes rather than their emotions. However, Libra's emotions are tied to Venus, and they have a strong emotional connection beneath the surface.

The challenge is that they both tend to talk about their feelings without fully experiencing them. True emotional depth in their relationship can be achieved when Libra follows Gemini on their adventures and when Gemini's love deepens to the point where words lose their significance.

Gemini & Libra Values (55%): Libra values consistency, responsibility, and reliability, while Gemini places a high value on creativity and intellectual strength. Their common ground lies in their appreciation for mental compatibility. Both being Air signs, they focus on their partner's mental attributes and the way they think. While their values may differ in other areas, they can connect through their shared intellectual interests.

Gemini & Libra Shared Activities (85%): Libra is adaptable when in love and is willing to engage in various activities to please their partner. They expect similar enthusiasm in return from their partner, which can sometimes drain their energy if not reciprocated. Gemini, on the other hand, doesn't prioritize following their partner's lead.

To enjoy shared activities, both partners need to manage their expectations, respect each other's boundaries, and be open to trying new and exciting experiences.

In summary, while Gemini and Libra may face some challenges, they have the potential for a fulfilling relationship. Libra's need for togetherness and Gemini's role as a teacher and a friend can complement each other. By understanding and respecting each other's unique qualities, they can build a strong and harmonious connection.

Compatibility Score: 78%

Gemini & Scorpio: A Complex and Challenging Connection

Gemini & Scorpio Sexual & Intimacy Compatibility (1%): When it comes to intimacy, Gemini and Scorpio face significant hurdles. Their sexual connection is hindered by the vast emotional gap between them. Gemini's superficiality and emotional detachment clash with Scorpio's deep and passionate nature. To have a satisfying sexual relationship, they would need strong support from other aspects of their natal charts.

Gemini & Scorpio Trust (5%): Trust is a complex issue in this relationship. Scorpio places a high premium on trust, demanding unwavering commitment and complete honesty. Gemini, however, struggles with consistency and often finds it challenging to maintain their word. This can lead to trust issues, especially if Scorpio has experienced betrayal in the past.

Gemini & Scorpio Communication And Intellect (20%): Gemini's natural ability to communicate and their inquisitive nature can initially captivate Scorpio. However, Scorpio's intense and profound discussions can veer into dark and depressive territories, which Gemini prefers to avoid. Scorpio may not see much value in Gemini's knowledge, potentially leading to conflicts. However, if they discover common interests, their conversations can be a source of inspiration.

Gemini & Scorpio Emotions (1%): Emotional compatibility is a significant challenge for this pair. If one partner falls deeply in love while the other remains emotionally distant, it creates dissatisfaction and tension. Synchronizing their emotional scales is a formidable task, and their best approach is to give without expecting reciprocation.

Gemini & Scorpio Values (20%): Both Gemini and Scorpio share an appreciation for intellectual strength and thoughtful insights. While they may have different values in other areas, they can find common ground in their shared interest in mental compatibility.

Gemini & Scorpio Shared Activities (40%): Both partners are open to change, although they approach it differently. Scorpio seeks profound life transformations, while Gemini craves a diverse range of experiences. Despite occasional disagreements due to their distinct outlooks, they can find excitement and personal growth through the activities they pursue together.

In summary, the relationship between Gemini and Scorpio is marked by complexity and challenges. They struggle to understand and connect with each other's personalities. However, if they fall deeply in love, they have the potential to complement each other and undergo personal growth by embracing their differences.

Compatibility Score: 15%

Gemini & Sagittarius: An Adventurous and Playful Duo

Gemini & Sagittarius Sexual & Intimacy Compatibility (90%): Gemini and Sagittarius approach sex with a lighthearted and carefree attitude. Their sexual connection is marked by childlike innocence and a lack of pressure. They revel in open communication and experience joy, creativity, and laughter in their sexual encounters. Sex is not the focal point of their relationship; instead, they seek a mental connection and a sense of purpose in their partnership.

Gemini & Sagittarius Trust (99%): Both Gemini and Sagittarius understand the need for personal freedom and may have multiple relationships simultaneously. This mutual understanding can lead to ultimate faithfulness, as the allure of secrecy and mystery fades. They build trust on foundations of mutual respect and play a game of trust that strengthens their bond.

Gemini & Sagittarius Communication And Intellect (99%): The intellectual connection between Gemini and Sagittarius is profound. They share an insatiable curiosity and inspire each other to explore various ideas and experiences.

While their mental connection is strong, they may fear the intensity of emotions that can emerge in their relationship. However, their optimism and eloquence will bring happiness and joy to everyone around them.

Gemini & Sagittarius Emotions (95%): Although neither Gemini nor Sagittarius are traditionally emotional signs, their connection often leads to an abundance of feelings. When they click, they discover a depth of emotion that may surprise them. It can be a captivating love story as long as they embrace and navigate their newfound emotions.

Gemini & Sagittarius Values (70%): Both signs value the importance of things making sense. Whether in their words or actions, everything must have a purpose and meaning. This shared value aligns their core beliefs and helps them find common ground.

Gemini & Sagittarius Shared Activities (99%): Their shared activities are boundless, and they embrace them with enthusiasm and laughter. As mutable signs, they understand each other's flexibility and adaptability. They are happy when together, and while they may appear overly carefree to others, they revel in their bliss.

In summary, Gemini and Sagittarius form an incredible couple, characterized by their innocence and mutual understanding. Their intellectual connection evolves into

deep emotions, and although fear may arise, their relationship holds immense potential for joy, adventure, and personal growth.

Compatibility Score: 92%

Gemini & Capricorn Compatibility

- **Sexual & Intimacy Compatibility (1%):** Gemini and Capricorn have vastly different approaches to sex. Gemini is open, talkative, and curious, while Capricorn sees sex as a more serious and less verbal experience.

- This stark contrast can make their sexual relationship challenging. Capricorn might find Gemini's approach to sex unconventional and carefree, while Gemini may view Capricorn as rigid and uncreative.

- In most cases, they may not be highly attracted to each other in this regard. For Gemini, the lack of depth and emotional connection in Capricorn can be a turn-off, while Capricorn could find Gemini too unconventional.

However, with clear communication and boundaries, they might find a way to make their sexual life work.

- **Trust (50%):** Capricorn values trust and faithfulness in a relationship, while Gemini's flirtatious nature may raise questions. Capricorn takes fidelity seriously and expects the same from their partner. Gemini's ease with bending the truth can be a source of concern for Capricorn. Capricorn tends to be thorough and can easily spot any inconsistencies in Gemini's stories. Still, Capricorn might trust their Gemini partner, but often based on their own interpretations of the truth.

- **Communication And Intellect (25%):** Gemini's ability to communicate with anyone contrasts with Capricorn's more serious and analytical approach to communication. They may struggle to see eye to eye on various subjects, as Capricorn seeks depth and meaning, while Gemini often engages in lighthearted conversations. However, they share a mutual curiosity about the world, which can serve as a bridge between their different approaches. If they can overcome their initial impressions of each other, they may find ways to appreciate their unique qualities and learn from each other.

- **Emotions (1%):** Both Gemini and Capricorn tend to be non-emotional signs, and their emotional connection can be limited. They might not spark strong emotions in each other and may find it challenging to connect on this level.

- **Values (5%):** Gemini values information, creativity, and communication, while Capricorn prioritizes stability, punctuality, and honesty. While they may appreciate each other's independence, their core values often diverge.

- **Shared Activities (10%):** Gemini's spontaneous approach to activities clashes with Capricorn's preference for planned, purposeful actions. While they both value constructive learning and problem-solving, their interests and motives usually lead them in different directions.

Summary (15%): Gemini and Capricorn are an unusual match. Although they both seek qualities the other possesses, they often fail to recognize them in each other. Gemini's need for depth and grounding may make Capricorn appear old-fashioned and uninspiring, while Capricorn's need for stability and seriousness may cause Gemini to see them as rigid and dull. In reality, if they can work on communication and understanding, they might discover that their differences could complement each other. Their unique qualities may be assets rather than liabilities, allowing them to reach their shared goals and build a meaningful relationship.

Gemini & Aquarius Compatibility

Sexual & Intimacy Compatibility (1%): A Unique Approach Gemini and Aquarius have a distinctive take on intimacy, often engaging in sexual experiences through verbal stimulation. Their sexual encounters are marked by a desire for freedom and a search for kindred spirits, allowing them to explore unconventional places and scenarios. Both value intelligence in their partners, seeking individuals with wit and substance. While their adaptability and open communication are strengths, their connection may lack deep emotional bonds, which could lead to drifting apart.

Trust (85%): Strong Foundation Trust is a cornerstone of their relationship. Aquarius and Gemini prioritize freedom and honesty, which forms the basis of their strong trust in each other. They have a unique way of trusting without resorting to lies, finding each other's quirks intriguing. Their relationship flourishes due to open, judgment-free communication, which further solidifies their trust.

Communication And Intellect (99%): Intellectual Stimulation Gemini and Aquarius engage in intellectually stimulating debates that captivate not only themselves but also those around them. They challenge each other's thoughts and ideas, embracing their differences. Gemini finds Aquarius's rational and humane belief system fascinating, while Aquarius appreciates Gemini's adaptability. Maintaining flexibility and aligning on life philosophies is crucial to prevent excessive talk without meaningful action.

Emotions (40%): Rational Companions Both Gemini and Aquarius possess a rational, non-emotional nature. They understand each other's need for emotional independence but may seek deeper emotional connections outside their relationship. Their bond is often more platonic than passionate, emphasizing shared intellectual interests.

Values (95%): Intellectual Alignment Intellect is at the core of their shared values. Aquarius's passion for humane beliefs aligns with Gemini's understanding, fostering a strong connection. However, differences can emerge when Aquarius places equal importance on freedom and equality, potentially leading to minor disagreements.

Shared Activities (99%): Thrilling Adventures Aquarius's ability to surprise and challenge Gemini makes their shared activities thrilling. They are adventurous, always ready to travel, explore, and embrace life's quirks. Movement is their primary shared activity, whether it involves driving miles for a unique ice cream flavor or engaging in various adventures, from clubbing to exploring kitchenware instructions.

Summary (85%): An Exciting Match with Room for Growth Gemini and Aquarius form an exciting match, driven by their shared intellectual interests and mutual respect for each other's uniqueness. To strengthen their relationship further, they must work on enhancing their emotional connection and non-verbal understanding, ensuring that their bond endures and continues to evolve.

Gemini & Pisces Compatibility

Sexual & Intimacy Compatibility (15%): *A Challenging Connection* Gemini's creativity in the bedroom clashes with Pisces' romantic approach to intimacy. While both signs may be initially attracted to each other due to shared ruling planets, they may struggle to connect on a deeper level. Gemini values casual encounters, while Pisces seeks profound emotional connections. For this sexual relationship to work, they need to ground themselves and communicate effectively.

Trust (1%): Trusting the Unspoken Trust can be a weak point in their relationship, as they have different ways of dealing with emotions and self-image issues. Their ability to sense each other's feelings can lead to a lack of trust. They may not communicate honestly with each other, and when they do, they often don't listen deeply. Their trust is built on superficial conversations rather than emotional understanding.

Communication And Intellect (20%): Surface-Level Connections Gemini and Pisces share lighthearted conversations, but their communication often lacks depth. They tend to idealize each other, which can lead to unrealistic expectations. If they delve into deeper conversations, conflicts may arise. They are more likely to have meaningful discussions when they share absolute emotional intimacy, akin to familial relationships.

Emotions (1%): Unmatched Emotional Levels Gemini is rational, while Pisces is deeply emotional. When they fall in love, their emotional frequencies rarely align. One partner usually has more genuine emotions than the other. This disparity can lead to unreturned love scenarios and cause challenges in their relationship.

Values (5%): Creativity Bonds Them While they have different priorities and values, one common bond is their appreciation for creativity. They both value someone's ability to create, albeit from different perspectives. Pisces provides inspiration and talent, while Gemini contributes resourcefulness and practicality in their creative endeavors.

Shared Activities (15%): A Need for Movement As mutable signs, Gemini and Pisces may engage in various activities due to their shared need for movement. Gemini can motivate Pisces to take action and make their dreams a reality. However, their interests can differ significantly, and they may struggle to maintain a deep connection in shared activities.

Summary (10%): Superficial Compatibility with Potential for

Growth Gemini and Pisces have a superficial, enjoyable relationship, often working well in social settings. However, their differences can be a source of hurt for Pisces. While they may not share the same long-term goals, there is potential for growth in their creative pursuits if Gemini truly listens to Pisces. Communication, deep understanding, and shared socialization are key to making this relationship work. They must strive for emotional intimacy to succeed in their quest for lasting love.

Gemini Man: A Lover's Guide

The Gemini Man

The Gemini man is a vibrant and lively personality, never allowing dull moments to creep into his life. He's an adventurer, a source of humor, and an ideal partner for someone who seeks energy, dynamism, and laughter.

You can find him at public gatherings, conferences, or even in the middle of traffic jams, always ready for a chat. His character is defined by dualism, making him both inconsistent and clever, which intriguingly draws others to him.

To capture his heart, you must be fun, stimulating, adventurous, laugh at his jokes, and be willing to learn from him every day. Despite his eloquent nature, he tends to avoid discussing emotions and prefers to see them displayed rather than spoken.

In the realm of intimacy, a Gemini man values variety, experimentation, and verbal connection. His sexual relationships require freedom of expression and fresh experiences to keep him engaged and interested.

Gemini Woman: A Lover's Guide

The Gemini Woman

Attracting a Gemini woman requires the ability to keep up with her dual nature. She can be passionate and gentle one moment, then aloof and distant the next. This duality arises from her innate inclination to maintain a safe distance from others, always prepared to dive into a carefree love story. She is passionate, witty, intellectual, and softly spoken, yet exceptionally open-minded and always eager to meet new people.

While a Gemini woman is not typically reserved, entering into a serious and committed relationship with her demands time and a great deal of patience. However, when she finds a partner who can satisfy her both intellectually and sexually, she might be the one to propose starting a family and building a future together, albeit in a unique manner. She's impressed by individuals who can teach her new things and provide insights she considers ingenious. Her sexual journey is a narrative she's willing to share but only with that one special person with whom she has established genuine intimacy.

Understanding the unique qualities and preferences of a Gemini man and woman is essential for forming meaningful and fulfilling relationships with them. Their lively and changeable nature makes them intriguing and dynamic partners.

"Geminis Unveiled: A Cosmic Journey into the Twins of the Zodiac"

Chapter 1: The Enigmatic Gemini - A Dual Personality Unveiled

Introduction:

The Gemini Zodiac Sign, symbolized by the Twins, is often regarded as one of the most enigmatic signs of the zodiac. Its association with duality and complexity has intrigued astrologers and enthusiasts alike for centuries. In this chapter, we embark on a journey to unveil the mysteries of the Gemini personality, exploring their unique characteristics and the enigmatic nature of this Air sign.

The Gemini Duality:

At the heart of the Gemini personality lies a profound duality that sets them apart from the other zodiac signs. Geminis are renowned for their ability to view the world from two different perspectives, often simultaneously. This duality is not a contradiction but rather a harmonious coexistence of opposing traits within the same individual.

The Twins:

The symbol of Gemini, the Twins, beautifully encapsulates this dual nature. These celestial siblings represent the adaptability, versatility, and the constant interplay of opposing characteristics within Geminis. They are like two sides of a coin, each offering a unique perspective on life. It is the dynamic synergy between these Twins that creates the complexity that is Gemini.

The Air Element:

In the realm of the zodiac, Gemini belongs to the Air element, sharing this status with fellow signs Libra and Aquarius. The influence of the Air element on Geminis is evident in their intellectual prowess, communication skills, and their insatiable thirst for knowledge.

The Air element endows them with the gift of analytical thinking, rationality, and a deep-seated desire to engage with the world on an intellectual level. Like a gentle breeze that carries the whispers of wisdom, Geminis are constantly seeking to gather information, exchange ideas, and communicate their findings with eloquence.

Mercury's Influence:

The ruling planet of Gemini is Mercury, and this celestial body plays a pivotal role in shaping their characteristics. Mercury is the planet of communication, travel, and intellect. It's the cosmic force behind their quick wit, agility of thought, and their natural ability to express themselves with precision.

Mercury's influence can be likened to a mental whirlwind, constantly churning out new ideas and insights. It gifts Geminis with an innate curiosity that drives them to explore, learn, and adapt to the ever-evolving world around them.

The Intellectual Explorers:

Geminis are natural intellectuals, driven by an insatiable curiosity to explore the world. They possess an innate intellectual agility that allows them to effortlessly absorb a broad spectrum of knowledge, making them lifelong learners and adept conversationalists.

In their quest for intellectual nourishment, Geminis often find themselves immersed in various topics, from science and literature to art and culture. They thrive in environments that encourage the exchange of ideas and the free flow of information.

Adaptability and Change:

One of Gemini's most remarkable qualities is their adaptability. They readily adjust to different situations and thrive on change. This characteristic is closely tied to their Air element, which encourages flexibility and an open-minded approach to life.

Geminis are the chameleons of the zodiac, seamlessly transitioning between different social circles and adapting to diverse environments. Their ability to embrace change is a testament to their resilience and their willingness to embrace the unknown.

Social Butterflies:

Geminis are known as social butterflies, effortlessly connecting with a wide array of people from all walks of life. Their sociable nature is an extension of their Air sign attributes, making them the life of any gathering. They are the individuals who light up a room with their infectious energy and captivating conversations.

The Gemini personality thrives on interactions and engaging with people who bring diverse perspectives and ideas to the table. They are often the ones who initiate conversations and keep the dialogue flowing. Their social versatility allows them to create meaningful connections with a multitude of individuals.

The Twins' Dark Side:

While Geminis possess a myriad of positive traits, their dual nature can also lead to inconsistencies and indecisiveness. It's important to understand that both sides of their personality coexist, and embracing the complexities of Geminis is essential to comprehending their true nature.

In their quest to explore the vast spectrum of life, Geminis may encounter moments of indecision and uncertainty.

Their dualism can sometimes lead to inner conflicts as they navigate between contrasting desires and viewpoints. This duality is a constant challenge for Geminis, pushing them to find harmony within themselves.

Conclusion:

The enigma of Gemini lies in their dual personality, which is a reflection of the Twins' symbol and the Air element's influence. In this chapter, we've merely scratched the surface of what makes Geminis unique. The subsequent chapters will delve deeper into their multifaceted character, offering a comprehensive understanding of this intriguing zodiac sign. The journey to uncover the essence of Gemini has only just begun.

Chapter 1: The Enigmatic Gemini - A Dual Personality Unveiled

Introduction:

The Gemini Zodiac Sign, symbolized by the Twins, is often regarded as one of the most enigmatic signs of the zodiac. Its association with duality and complexity has intrigued astrologers and enthusiasts alike for centuries. In this chapter, we embark on a journey to unveil the mysteries of the Gemini personality, exploring their unique characteristics and the enigmatic nature of this Air sign.

The Gemini Duality:

At the heart of the Gemini personality lies a profound duality that sets them apart from the other zodiac signs. Geminis are renowned for their ability to view the world from two different perspectives, often simultaneously. This duality is not a contradiction but rather a harmonious coexistence of opposing traits within the same individual.

The Twins:

The symbol of Gemini, the Twins, beautifully encapsulates this dual nature. These celestial siblings represent the adaptability, versatility, and the constant interplay of opposing characteristics within Geminis. They are like two sides of a coin, each offering a unique perspective on life. It is the dynamic synergy between these Twins that creates the complexity that is Gemini.

The Air Element:

In the realm of the zodiac, Gemini belongs to the Air element, sharing this status with fellow signs Libra and Aquarius. The influence of the Air element on Geminis is evident in their intellectual prowess, communication skills, and their insatiable thirst for knowledge.

The Air element endows them with the gift of analytical thinking, rationality, and a deep-seated desire to engage with the world on an intellectual level. Like a gentle breeze that carries the whispers of wisdom, Geminis are constantly seeking to gather information, exchange ideas, and communicate their findings with eloquence.

Mercury's Influence:

The ruling planet of Gemini is Mercury, and this celestial body plays a pivotal role in shaping their characteristics. Mercury is the planet of communication, travel, and intellect. It's the cosmic force behind their quick wit, agility of thought, and their natural ability to express themselves with precision.

Mercury's influence can be likened to a mental whirlwind, constantly churning out new ideas and insights. It gifts Geminis with an innate curiosity that drives them to explore, learn, and adapt to the ever-evolving world around them.

The Intellectual Explorers:

Geminis are natural intellectuals, driven by an insatiable curiosity to explore the world. They possess an innate intellectual agility that allows them to effortlessly absorb a broad spectrum of knowledge, making them lifelong learners and adept conversationalists.

In their quest for intellectual nourishment, Geminis often find themselves immersed in various topics, from science and literature to art and culture. They thrive in environments that encourage the exchange of ideas and the free flow of information.

Adaptability and Change:

One of Gemini's most remarkable qualities is their adaptability. They readily adjust to different situations and thrive on change. This characteristic is closely tied to their Air element, which encourages flexibility and an open-minded approach to life.

Geminis are the chameleons of the zodiac, seamlessly transitioning between different social circles and adapting to diverse environments. Their ability to embrace change is a testament to their resilience and their willingness to embrace the unknown.

Social Butterflies:

Geminis are known as social butterflies, effortlessly connecting with a wide array of people from all walks of life. Their sociable nature is an extension of their Air sign attributes, making them the life of any gathering. They are the individuals who light up a room with their infectious energy and captivating conversations.

The Gemini personality thrives on interactions and engaging with people who bring diverse perspectives and ideas to the table. They are often the ones who initiate conversations and keep the dialogue flowing. Their social versatility allows them to create meaningful connections with a multitude of individuals.

The Twins' Dark Side:

While Geminis possess a myriad of positive traits, their dual nature can also lead to inconsistencies and indecisiveness. It's important to understand that both sides of their personality coexist, and embracing the complexities of Geminis is essential to comprehending their true nature.

In their quest to explore the vast spectrum of life, Geminis may encounter moments of indecision and uncertainty. Their dualism can sometimes lead to inner conflicts as they navigate between contrasting desires and viewpoints. This duality is a constant challenge for

Geminis, pushing them to find harmony within themselves.

Conclusion:

The enigma of Gemini lies in their dual personality, which is a reflection of the Twins' symbol and the Air element's influence. In this chapter, we've merely scratched the surface of what makes Geminis unique. The subsequent chapters will delve deeper into their multifaceted character, offering a comprehensive understanding of this intriguing zodiac sign. The journey to uncover the essence of Gemini has only just begun.

Chapter 2: The Twins' Origins - Mythological Insights into Gemini

Introduction:

The enigmatic nature of Gemini extends beyond its astrological attributes. To truly understand this multifaceted zodiac sign, we must explore the rich tapestry of mythology that weaves its influence. In this chapter, we venture into the realm of ancient myths to uncover the origins of the Twins and the celestial forces that shaped the Gemini personality.

Castor and Pollux: The Divine Twins:

The mythological roots of Gemini find their expression in the story of Castor and Pollux, the legendary Gemini Twins. These divine siblings hail from Greek and Roman mythology, where they embody the dual nature of the zodiac sign.

Castor, the mortal son of Tyndareus, represents the earthly and physical aspect of the Twins. He was known for his exceptional horsemanship and combat skills. Pollux, on the other hand, was the immortal son of Zeus. He symbolizes the celestial and spiritual dimension of Gemini. As twins, they shared an inseparable bond, showcasing the dynamic interplay of contrasting elements.

The Immortal and the Mortal:

The myth of Castor and Pollux is a poignant reflection of the dualism inherent in Gemini. Castor, as a mortal, signifies the human experience with its fleeting nature and physical limitations. In contrast, Pollux's immortality represents the eternal and spiritual aspect of the Gemini personality.

The Twins' story is a reminder that Geminis are often torn between the desire for earthly experiences and the pursuit of intellectual and spiritual growth. This duality is at the core of their personality, driving them to explore both the material and the ethereal.

Sibling Synergy:

Castor and Pollux's unity in mythology showcases the harmonious coexistence of opposing traits within Geminis. They were not rivals but allies, complementing each other's strengths. This unity is reflective of the way Geminis navigate their dual nature, finding balance and synergy between their contrasting qualities.

Geminis understand that their duality is not a source of conflict but a unique blend of traits that enhances their life journey. Like the Twins of old, they recognize the power of collaboration between the physical and the spiritual.

Mercury's Role:

In the myth of Castor and Pollux, the planet Mercury's influence is evident. Mercury, the ruling planet of Gemini, was the messenger of the gods in Roman mythology. He facilitated communication and the exchange of knowledge, a role that mirrors the intellectual and communicative prowess of Geminis.

Mercury's presence in this myth reinforces the idea that Geminis are destined to be messengers, conveyors of ideas, and seekers of knowledge. They inherit Mercury's agile mind and the capacity to bridge the gap between the mortal and the divine.

The Gemini Constellation:

The constellation of Gemini, bearing the same name as the zodiac sign, is a prominent feature in the night sky. It consists of two bright stars, Castor and Pollux, representing the divine Twins. These stars have fascinated astronomers and stargazers for centuries.

The Gemini constellation's presence in the heavens serves as a constant reminder of the Twins' enduring legacy. It inspires Geminis to reach for the stars, both figuratively and literally, as they explore the vast realm of ideas and experiences.

Conclusion:

The myth of Castor and Pollux provides profound insights into the origins of the Gemini Twins. Their story is a testament to the harmony of opposites, the unity of mortal and immortal, and the enduring legacy of duality. As we continue our journey into the enigmatic world of Geminis, we'll uncover how these mythological roots continue to shape their dynamic personality and inspire their quest for knowledge and balance.

Chapter 3: Geminis in the Modern World - Personality Traits and Characteristics

Introduction:

In our exploration of Geminis, we transition from the realm of myth to the realities of the modern world. Geminis are not confined to ancient stories and celestial symbolism; they walk among us, bringing their unique traits and characteristics to life. In this chapter, we delve into the multifaceted nature of Geminis, dissecting their personality traits, strengths, and weaknesses.

The Charming Communicators:

Geminis are renowned for their exceptional communication skills. They possess the gift of gab and have an innate ability to engage with people from all walks of life. This charm is a result of their ruling planet, Mercury, which governs not only communication but also intellect. Geminis are often the life of the party, effortlessly keeping conversations flowing.

Strengths:

1. **Gentle:** Geminis are known for their gentle and adaptable nature. They can easily adjust to various social situations, making them approachable and empathetic.

2. **Affectionate:** Beneath their intellectual exterior, Geminis are deeply affectionate individuals. They value personal connections and aren't afraid to express their love and care for others.

3. **Curious:** Geminis possess an insatiable curiosity about the world. They're constantly seeking new experiences, knowledge, and intellectual stimulation. This trait fuels their quest for personal growth.

4. **Adaptable:** Adaptability is a hallmark of the Gemini personality. They can seamlessly transition from one role

to another, making them versatile and resourceful individuals.

5. Ability to Learn Quickly and Exchange Ideas: Geminis have a remarkable capacity to absorb information rapidly and share their ideas with enthusiasm. They thrive in educational and creative environments.

Weaknesses:

1. Nervous: The same intellectual energy that drives Geminis can also make them prone to nervousness. They may overanalyze situations and struggle with anxiety.

2. Inconsistent: Geminis' dual nature can lead to inconsistency in their actions and decisions. They may have difficulty committing to long-term plans.

3. Indecisive: Their tendency to weigh multiple options can make Geminis indecisive. They may find it challenging to make choices, especially when faced with complex decisions.

Gemini Likes:

1. **Music:** Geminis often have a deep appreciation for music in its various forms. They find solace and inspiration in melodies and rhythms.

2. **Books:** Intellectual stimulation is vital for Geminis, and books provide an endless source of knowledge and ideas.

3. **Magazines:** Magazines, with their bite-sized information and diverse content, align with Geminis' quick and curious minds.

4. **Chats with Nearly Anyone:** Geminis thrive on social interactions. They are not selective about their conversational partners and can strike up engaging discussions with nearly anyone.

5. **Short Trips Around the Town:** Geminis have an adventurous spirit, and

short trips provide them with the excitement of exploration and discovery.

Gemini Dislikes:

1. Being Alone: Solitude is a challenge for Geminis. They thrive on social connections and may feel uneasy when left to their own devices.

2. Being Confined: Geminis cherish their freedom and resist confinement in any form, be it physical or intellectual.

3. Repetition and Routine: Predictability and monotonous routines are anathema to Geminis. They seek variety and change in their daily lives.

Conclusion:

In this chapter, we've dissected the multifaceted personality of Geminis. Their strengths, such as their gentle nature, curiosity, and adaptability, make them charming communicators and engaging individuals. However, they grapple with nervousness, inconsistency, and indecision due to their dual nature. Understanding these traits is crucial as we navigate the intriguing world of Geminis and their interactions with the people and experiences that surround them. In the next chapter, we'll explore the influences of the air element and Mercury, their ruling planet, on the Gemini personality.

Chapter 4: The Air Element and Mercury's Influence on Gemini

Introduction:

In the previous chapter, we delved deep into the intricate personality of Geminis, uncovering their strengths and weaknesses. Now, we venture further into the cosmos to unravel the astrological forces that shape Geminis—the element of Air and the influence of their ruling planet, Mercury. These celestial components add unique dimensions to the Gemini personality.

The Air Element:

Air is one of the four classical elements and represents the intellectual realm. It is associated with communication, thought, and the exchange of ideas. Geminis belong to the Air signs, along with Libra and Aquarius. This element endows them with intellectual prowess and a penchant for social interaction.

Air signs are characterized by their agility in adapting to various situations and their ability to form connections with others through words and ideas. For Geminis, this element is akin to their lifeblood, driving their insatiable curiosity and knack for conversation.

Mercury: The Messenger of the Gods:

In the realm of astrology, each zodiac sign is ruled by one or more celestial bodies. Geminis are under the governance of Mercury, the planet associated with communication, intellect, and travel. Mercury is often referred to as the messenger of the gods, as it facilitates the exchange of information and ideas.

The influence of Mercury on Geminis is profound. It amplifies their innate communicative skills, making them eloquent and persuasive. This planet is also linked to adaptability, a quality that Geminis possess in abundance. They can effortlessly transition between roles, adopting new perspectives and ideas with ease.

The Gemini Personality under Air and Mercury:

1. Intellectual Agility: Geminis are intellectual powerhouses, thanks to the Air element and Mercury's influence. They possess an agile mind that thrives on the exploration of new ideas, concepts, and information.

2. Verbal   Dexterity: Communication is at the core of the Gemini personality. They have an innate talent for conveying their thoughts and ideas with precision and eloquence.

3. Social Butterflies: The Air element's sociability is heightened in Geminis. They excel in social settings, effortlessly forming connections and engaging in captivating conversations.

4. Adaptability: Mercury's influence enhances Geminis' adaptability. They can pivot and adjust to changing circumstances, making them versatile and resourceful individuals.

5. Curiosity: The combination of the Air element and Mercury's influence fuels Geminis' insatiable curiosity. They are perpetually inquisitive, seeking to expand their knowledge and experiences.

Conclusion:

In this chapter, we've ventured into the realm of astrological forces that shape Geminis. The Air element and the influence of Mercury play a pivotal role in enhancing their communicative skills, adaptability, and intellectual agility. These cosmic influences provide a unique backdrop to the multifaceted Gemini personality, adding depth and richness to their interactions with the world. In the following chapters, we'll explore the compatibility of Geminis with other zodiac signs, their love and relationships, and their professional pursuits.

Chapter 5: Gemini's Interactions with Other Zodiac Signs

Introduction:

In the previous chapters, we've dissected the intricate elements that make up a Gemini's personality—their dual nature, strengths and weaknesses, and the astrological forces of Air and Mercury. Now, we shift our focus to one of the most fascinating aspects of astrology: how Geminis interact with individuals of other zodiac signs. The interplay of energies and characteristics when different signs come together can result in unique dynamics and relationships.

The Zodiac Wheel:

The zodiac wheel consists of twelve signs, each with its distinct personality traits, strengths, and quirks. For Geminis, understanding how they relate to individuals from other signs can provide valuable insights into their personal and social life. To do this, we'll explore

Gemini's compatibility with each sign of the zodiac.

Aries (March 21 - April 19):

Geminis and Aries share a sense of adventure and curiosity. They both thrive on new experiences and intellectual stimulation. While they may have their disagreements, their shared enthusiasm often helps them overcome differences.

Taurus (April 20 - May 20):

Gemini's constant need for change can clash with Taurus's desire for stability. Taurus may find Gemini's unpredictability unsettling, while Gemini might feel stifled by Taurus's routine-oriented approach.

Cancer (June 21 - July 22):

Geminis and Cancers operate in very different emotional realms. Geminis value intellectual connections, while Cancers prioritize emotional bonds.

Understanding and respecting each other's needs is key to a harmonious relationship.

Leo (July 23 - August 22):

Both Gemini and Leo love the spotlight and are often the life of the party. Their outgoing personalities can make for a vibrant and dynamic partnership. However, they should be mindful of ego clashes.

Virgo (August 23 - September 22):

Gemini's adaptability and Virgo's practicality can create a balanced relationship. Virgo's attention to detail complements Gemini's big-picture thinking. Together, they can achieve their goals efficiently.

Libra (September 23 - October 22):

Both signs belong to the Air element, which fosters excellent communication. Geminis and Libras share an intellectual connection and a love for socializing. They are often drawn to each other's charm and wit.

Scorpio (October 23 - November 21):

Gemini's lightheartedness can clash with Scorpio's intensity. While they may be initially attracted to each other's mystery, maintaining a relationship requires a deeper understanding of their differences.

Sagittarius (November 22 - December 21):

Geminis and Sagittarians are natural explorers. They both crave adventure and intellectual growth. Their shared love for travel and new experiences can make for an exciting partnership.

Capricorn (December 22 - January 19):

Capricorns are practical and goal-oriented, which can sometimes clash with Gemini's more spontaneous nature. However, they can learn from each other—Capricorn can teach Gemini discipline, while Gemini can infuse some spontaneity into Capricorn's life.

Aquarius (January 20 - February 18):

Both signs belong to the Air element, fostering a strong mental connection. Geminis and Aquarians appreciate each other's innovative thinking and thirst for knowledge. They can engage in stimulating conversations and share intellectual pursuits.

Pisces (February 19 - March 20):

Gemini's rationality may clash with Pisces's emotional depth. Finding common ground may require effort, but when they do, they can balance each other's strengths and weaknesses.

Conclusion:

In this chapter, we've explored how Geminis interact with individuals of different zodiac signs. While each relationship is unique, understanding the potential dynamics and challenges between Geminis and other signs can lead to more harmonious and fulfilling connections. As we delve deeper into the world of Gemini's relationships, we'll explore their love life, family dynamics, and friendships in the chapters that follow.

Chapter 6: Gemini in Love

Introduction:

Love is a complex and profound aspect of human life, and for Geminis, it's no exception. In this chapter, we'll delve into the world of Gemini in love, exploring their romantic tendencies, desires, and potential challenges when it comes to matters of the heart.

The Duality of Love:

Geminis are often seen as enigmatic lovers because of their dual nature. On one hand, they can be passionate and deeply engaged in their relationships, showering their partners with affection, wit, and charm. On the other hand, they might experience moments of aloofness, leaving their partners puzzled and yearning for more.

Communication is Key:

For Geminis, communication is the cornerstone of a successful relationship. They are natural conversationalists and enjoy sharing their thoughts and ideas with their partners. This desire for intellectual engagement means that they appreciate partners who can hold their own in stimulating conversations.

Freedom and Independence:

Geminis value their independence and freedom, and this extends to their love lives. They are drawn to partners who understand and respect their need for personal space and exploration. A partner who attempts to stifle their freedom or is overly possessive may find it challenging to win a Gemini's heart.

Variety and Spontaneity:

Geminis thrive on variety and spontaneity. They enjoy trying new things, exploring new places, and embarking on adventures with their partners. A routine or stagnant relationship can leave them feeling bored and unfulfilled.

Challenges in Love:

While Geminis bring excitement and intellectual stimulation to their relationships, they can also face challenges. Their occasional emotional detachment may leave their partners yearning for deeper emotional connections. Additionally, their flirtatious nature can lead to misunderstandings and jealousy if not communicated openly.

Compatibility and Love Matches:

Geminis can form successful relationships with a variety of zodiac signs. However, some signs align more naturally with their qualities and preferences. Sagittarius and Aquarius, for example, are known to be great love matches for Geminis due to their shared love of adventure and intellectual pursuits.

Conclusion:

In the world of love, Geminis are unique and multifaceted individuals. Their dual nature can make them both captivating and puzzling partners. By embracing their love for communication, freedom, and variety, they can forge deep and meaningful connections with compatible partners. In the chapters that follow, we'll explore Gemini's relationships with family and friends, providing a comprehensive view of their social life and interpersonal dynamics.

Chapter 7: Gemini's Relationships with Family and Friends

Introduction:

While much has been said about Gemini's love life, their interactions with family and friends are equally fascinating and complex. In this chapter, we'll explore the multifaceted relationships that Geminis share with their family members and the friendships they cultivate.

Family Dynamics:

Gemini's relationships with family members are marked by their ability to adapt to various roles and situations. They often find themselves as the communicators, bridging gaps between family members, and keeping the atmosphere light-hearted with their wit and charm.

Sibling Bonds:

Geminis tend to have a playful and chatty nature, which can make them popular among their siblings. Sibling bonds are usually filled with laughter and communication, making it easy for Geminis to connect with their brothers and sisters.

Parental Relationships:

Gemini's relationship with their parents can be diverse. They may see their parents as a source of guidance and wisdom or, in some cases, they could have a more independent approach to life, valuing their freedom. It's not uncommon for Geminis to have a strong intellectual connection with at least one of their parents.

Friendships:

Geminis are known for their extensive social circles and the ability to make friends wherever they go. They thrive in social settings and enjoy the diversity of personalities in their friendships. Their friends appreciate their wit, curiosity, and their willingness to try new things.

The Gift of Gab:

Communication is the cornerstone of Gemini's friendships. They are the friends who keep the group chat alive with memes, news articles, and endless conversations. Their friends often turn to them for advice and engaging discussions.

Adaptable and Fun:

Geminis are adaptable and can easily switch from one group of friends to another. They enjoy gatherings, parties, and events, bringing their cheerful and light-hearted nature to every occasion.

Challenges in Friendships:

While Gemini's sociable nature is an asset in friendships, it can sometimes lead to challenges. They may struggle with deeper emotional connections and may find it hard to be fully present in each friendship. Their flirtatious tendencies can also lead to misunderstandings with friends.

Conclusion:

Gemini's social life is a rich tapestry of family and friends, marked by their natural ability to connect with others and keep things exciting. In this chapter, we've explored their dynamics with family members and the traits that make them sought-after friends. The next chapter will delve into Gemini's career and work preferences, shedding light on their professional aspirations and challenges in the workplace.

Chapter 8: Gemini's Career and Work Preferences

Introduction:

Gemini individuals bring their versatile and intellectual qualities to the workplace, making them valuable assets in a range of careers. In this chapter, we'll explore Gemini's career inclinations, their work preferences, and how they handle professional challenges.

Intellectual Powerhouses:

Geminis are known for their intellectual prowess and their ability to grasp new concepts quickly. This quality makes them ideal candidates for careers that require mental agility and adaptability.

Versatile Career Choices:

One of Gemini's standout characteristics is their versatility. They often find success in a variety of fields, including journalism, writing, public relations, teaching, sales, and even acting. Their love for communication and storytelling can lead them to excel in these areas.

Adaptable in the Workplace:

Geminis thrive in dynamic work environments where they can adapt to changing situations. They often embrace new challenges and are quick to find innovative solutions. Their flexibility allows them to take on different roles within a company.

Curiosity and Problem-Solving:

Gemini's insatiable curiosity serves them well in their careers. They are not afraid to ask questions, research thoroughly, and explore new avenues to solve problems. This makes them valuable team members and leaders.

Challenges in the Workplace:

While Geminis have numerous strengths, they also face challenges in the workplace. Their penchant for multitasking can lead to scattered focus and unfinished projects. They may also struggle with routine tasks, craving variety and mental stimulation.

Work-Life Balance:

Maintaining a healthy work-life balance can be a challenge for Geminis. Their dedication to their careers and their desire to learn and experience new things can sometimes overshadow personal time and relationships.

Conclusion:

Geminis are the intellectual powerhouses of the zodiac, using their versatile nature and curiosity to excel in a range of careers. This chapter has shed light on their adaptable approach to the workplace, their problem-solving abilities, and the challenges they might encounter. The next chapter delves into

Gemini's approach to health and well-being, highlighting how they can maintain their energy and vitality.

Chapter 9: Gemini's Health and Well-Being

Introduction:

Gemini individuals bring their lively and curious nature to the realm of health and well-being. In this chapter, we will explore how Geminis approach their physical and mental health, their common health concerns, and tips for maintaining vitality.

Energetic Souls:

Geminis are known for their boundless energy and enthusiasm. They often have a zest for life that keeps them on the move and seeking new experiences. However, this vibrant energy can sometimes lead to restlessness and the need for effective stress management.

Mental Well-Being:

Gemini's mind is their greatest asset, but it can also be a source of stress. They tend to overthink and analyze situations, which can lead to anxiety and mental fatigue. Finding healthy outlets for mental energy, such as meditation or creative hobbies, can greatly benefit their well-being.

Physical Activity:

Exercise is essential for Geminis to release pent-up energy. They may find enjoyment in a variety of activities, from team sports to yoga or dancing. Maintaining a regular fitness routine helps them manage stress and stay physically fit.

Healthy Eating:

Geminis are often open to trying new foods and enjoy variety in their diet. They should focus on a balanced and nutritious diet to fuel their active lifestyles. Incorporating fruits, vegetables, and whole grains can help support their physical and mental vitality.

Stress Management:

Geminis may encounter stress due to their overactive minds and restless nature. Effective stress management techniques include mindfulness, relaxation exercises, and seeking professional help if needed. Finding a creative outlet for self-expression can also be therapeutic.

Common Health Concerns:

Geminis should be mindful of respiratory issues, as they are associated with the lungs. Regular check-ups and respiratory exercises can help maintain lung health. Additionally, they should pay attention to their nervous system and mental well-being to prevent stress-related ailments.

Balancing Act:

Maintaining a balance between mental and physical well-being is crucial for Geminis. They must learn to slow down and enjoy moments of relaxation while also indulging their natural curiosity and desire for exploration.

Conclusion:

Geminis' energetic and curious nature makes them proactive in managing their health and well-being. This chapter has provided insights into their approach to physical and mental wellness, highlighting the importance of balance and stress management. The following chapter delves into Gemini's relationships, shedding light on their compatibility with other zodiac signs and their approach to love and friendship.

Chapter 10: Gemini's Relationships

Introduction:

In this chapter, we explore the intricate world of Gemini's relationships. Geminis are known for their adaptability, communication skills, and social nature. We'll delve into how these qualities affect their connections with others, both in friendships and romantic partnerships.

Social Butterflies:

Geminis are social creatures by nature. They thrive in social settings, often making friends easily and enjoying the company of diverse individuals. They have a natural charm and can strike up conversations with anyone, making them the life of the party.

Friendships:

Geminis value friendships and enjoy having a wide circle of acquaintances. They are the friends who keep you entertained with their stories and wit. However, their adaptability can sometimes make it seem like they have many acquaintances but few deep friendships.

Communication in Friendships:

Communication is at the core of Gemini friendships. They love to chat, share ideas, and keep in touch. Text messages, phone calls, and social media are their playgrounds for staying connected. Geminis are the friends who always have something interesting to talk about.

Gemini in Love:

Geminis' romantic relationships are filled with excitement and variety. They seek partners who can match their intellectual curiosity and keep up with their fast-paced lives. Geminis fall in love with the mind as much as the heart.

Challenges in Love:

While Geminis are passionate lovers, they can sometimes struggle with commitment and settling into a routine. Their fear of being tied down or feeling bored can lead to challenges in long-term relationships. They need partners who understand their need for freedom.

Compatibility:

Geminis find compatibility with signs that appreciate their communicative nature and love of adventure. Sagittarius and Aquarius are often great matches, as they share these qualities. Libra and Aries can also provide exciting connections for Geminis.

Friendships vs. Romance:

Geminis often blur the lines between friendship and romance. They may start relationships as friends and gradually transition into romantic partners. Their romantic partners often become their best friends, sharing not just love but a strong intellectual connection.

Conclusion:

Geminis are social butterflies who thrive in the realm of relationships. Their adaptability and communication skills make them sought-after friends and exciting romantic partners. In the next chapter, we'll explore the careers and life paths that align with Gemini's versatile nature and intellectual pursuits.

Conclusion:

In this final chapter, we bring our journey through the world of Geminis to a close. We've explored the multifaceted personality of Geminis, their strengths, weaknesses, relationships, and life paths. Let's take a moment to summarize the unique qualities that make Geminis stand out.

Geminis are the embodiment of duality. They are the yin and yang of the zodiac, representing the light and dark, the serious and playful, the restless and calm. Their adaptability and quick wit are their superpowers, allowing them to thrive in various aspects of life. Their love for communication and learning fuels their journey of exploration.

This book has been an invitation to celebrate and embrace your inner Gemini, whether you are a Gemini yourself or have a Gemini in your life.

Their ever-curious and adaptable nature is a reminder that life is a journey of discovery, and change is the only constant. Embrace the duality within you and find beauty in the contradictions.

Appendix:

To continue your exploration of Geminis and astrology, we've compiled a list of additional resources, including recommended books, websites, and astrological tools. These resources can help you delve deeper into the fascinating world of Geminis and gain a better understanding of the zodiac.

Index:

For easy reference, we've included a comprehensive index to help you navigate this book and find specific topics of interest quickly.

Author's Note:

As the author of this book, I've had the privilege of delving into the world of Geminis and sharing insights and knowledge with you. I hope you've found this journey enlightening and entertaining. I encourage you to embrace the qualities that make Geminis unique and to continue exploring the wonders of astrology.

In closing, I invite you to approach life with the same curiosity and adaptability that Geminis embody. The world is a vast and ever-changing place, and there's always something new to discover. Just like a Gemini, be open to change, relish in the duality of your nature, and never stop seeking knowledge and adventure.

Thank you for joining me on this exploration of the Gemini zodiac sign. May your journey be filled with joy, laughter, and a lifelong quest for understanding the world and yourself.

Thank You!

Dear Reader,

As we come to the end of this journey through the captivating world of Geminis, we want to extend our heartfelt gratitude to you. Thank you for joining us in exploring the diverse and intriguing realm of this zodiac sign.

We hope you've enjoyed getting to know Geminis, understanding their multifaceted nature, and appreciating the beauty of duality that defines them. Just like Geminis, this book aimed to be adaptable, offering insights, stories, and knowledge that resonate with your curiosity.

If you've found this book illuminating and wish to explore the other zodiac signs, we invite you to search for the works of Daniel Sanjurjo. Each zodiac sign has its own unique characteristics, and you'll find a dedicated book for every sign, crafted with the same passion and dedication.

Thank you once again for embarking on this astrological adventure with us. We hope you continue your exploration of the stars and the fascinating world of astrology.

Wishing you a life filled with curiosity, adaptability, and the joy of discovery.

Warm regards,

Daniel Sanjurjo

danielsanjurjo47@gmail.com

Contact Us

Thank You,

Dear Reader

W e extend our sincere thanks to you, dear readers, for embarking on this astrological journey with us. Your curiosity, engagement, and trust have made this exploration of the Zodiac sign Cancer all the more fulfilling.

In these pages, we have delved into the essence of the Cancer sign, unveiling its secrets, traits, and the horoscope for 2024. We've ventured through the depths of emotion, explored the intricacies of relationships, and discovered the likes and dislikes of a Cancer individual. All of this would not have been possible without your interest and presence.

Your quest for knowledge and self-discovery is what fuels our passion for astrology, and we are grateful to have been your guides in this cosmic voyage. We hope that the insights and wisdom shared in these pages serve as a guiding light in your life.

We invite you to explore our other books, each dedicated to a unique Zodiac sign and various aspects of astrology. Whether you seek to deepen your understanding of the stars or uncover the mysteries of other signs, you'll find a wealth of knowledge waiting for you.

Should you have any questions, insights, or simply wish to connect with us, please don't hesitate to reach out.

You can contact us via **WhatsApp at +1 829-205-5456** or **email us at** danielsanjurjo47@gmail.com.

May the stars continue to shine brightly on your path, and may your journey through the Zodiac signs be filled with enlightenment, growth, and harmony. **Sincerely Daniel Sanjurjo**

Did you love Cancer Zodiac Sign 2024? Then you should read The Dreams Interpretation Book[1] by Daniel Sanjurjo!

2

☐ Unlock the Secrets of Dreams with "Dreamscape Chronicles: A Journey into the World of Dreams"

☐ Are you ready to embark on a profound dream interpretation journey that will unveil the hidden meanings of your dreams, offering insights into your inner self, personal growth, and self-discovery? "Dreamscape Chronicles" is your definitive guide to navigating the enigmatic landscapes of the subconscious mind.

☐ Explore the Depths of Dream Analysis: Delve into the

intricate world of dream interpretation, where the symbols and stories of the night come alive. From common dreams to the mysteries of the mind, this book unravels the symbolism and significance of your dreamscapes.

☐ Illuminate Your Path: Discover how dreams can inspire your creativity, provide therapeutic insights, and awaken your inner desires. This book serves as

your compass, guiding you through the rich tapestry of dreams and helping you harness their potential.

☐ Key Topics Explored: Uncover the significance of

dream symbolism, the role of
common dream themes, and the
influence of pioneers like
Sigmund

Freud in understanding the profound
landscapes of the dreamer's mind.

Are you ready to embark on a journey
through the dreamer's world? "Dreamscape
Chronicles" is your passport to the
boundless landscapes of your own mind.
Explore, interpret, and awaken to the
possibilities hidden within your dreams.

Unlock the mysteries of your dreams
and start your journey of self-discovery
today!

Also by Daniel Sanjurjo

Zodiaco

Piscis 2024: Un Viaje Celestial

Zodiac world

Aries Revealed 2024

Taurus 2024 Leo 2024

Gemini 2024

Cancer Zodiac Sign 2024

Virgo 2024

Scorpio 2024

Sagittarius 2024 Horoscope

Capricorn Unveiled: A Cosmic Guide to 2024

Aquarius Horoscope 2024

Standalone

The Dreams Interpretation Book

About the Author

Daniel Sanjurjo is a passionate author who delves into the realms of astrology and self-help. With a gift for exploring the celestial and the human psyche, Daniel's books are celestial journeys of self-discovery and personal growth. Join the cosmic odyssey with this insightful writer.